GETTING
NAKED

ALSO BY HARLAN COHEN

*The Naked Roommate: And 107 Other Issues You
Might Run Into in College*

*The Happiest Kid on Campus: A Parent's Guide to the Very Best
College Experience (for You and Your Child)*

*Dad's Pregnant Too!: Expectant fathers, expectant mothers, new
dads, and new moms share advice, tips, and stories about all the
surprises, questions, and joys ahead . . .*

GETTING
NAKED

....

FIVE STEPS
to Finding the
Love of Your Life
(While Fully Clothed
& Totally Sober)

....

HARLAN COHEN

To everyone who has ever written to me,
your questions ultimately revealed the answers.
This book is my answer to you.

And to Stephanie,
the best naked date ever.
I adore you.

www.stmartins.com

Design by Susan Walsh

Library of Congress Cataloging-in-Publication Data

Cohen, Harlan, 1973–
      Getting naked : five steps to finding the love of your life (while fully
   clothed & totally sober) / Harlan Cohen.
         p. cm.
      ISBN 978-0-312-61178-1 (trade pbk.)
      ISBN 978-1-4299-2695-9 (e-book)
   1. Dating (social customs).   2. Mate selection.   I. Title.
   HQ801.C633 2012
   306.73—dc23

                                                            2011045136

First Edition: April 2012

10   9   8   7   6   5   4   3   2   1

Contents

PART II
The Getting Naked Experiment: 5 Steps to Finding the
Love of Your Life (While Fully Clothed & Totally Sober)

Before Step 1

◀ • ▶

THE PHILOSOPHY OF GETTING NAKED

Love and life are 90 percent amazing and 10 percent bullshit. Too many times the 10 percent bullshit consumes 100 percent of our time. *Getting Naked* will help keep the 10 percent from taking up 100 percent of your time. And that will leave a lot more time to live, love, and have the time of your life.

THIS BOOK IS WRITTEN FOR . . .

SINGLE PEOPLE

Whether you've always been single or recently become single, *Getting Naked* will give you the power to find hundreds of lovers (note: you don't need to sleep with them all) or just one who you can spend the rest of your life loving.

PEOPLE IN RELATIONSHIPS

Getting Naked will help you understand exactly how you got into your relationships; why you or your partner struggle to communicate within your relationship; how to get the most out of your relationship; or how to find the confidence and courage to move on and find a happier, healthier, and more fulfilling relationship.

EVERYONE

Getting Naked is written for people of all ages, regions, religions, and sexual orientations. It's intended for women looking for men, men looking for women, women looking for women, men and women looking for two or three men and women to be with at the same time . . . (although, that's not the intended goal).

THE NAKED TRUTH ABOUT GETTING NAKED

I had to write this book. Not writing it would have been extremely selfish. It would have been like knowing the world's greatest secret and keeping it all to myself. And that's just *very* wrong. I'm not selfish.

I'm so relieved to share this with you. For more than seventeen years, people have been sharing their deepest darkest secrets with me. And for years, I've personally benefitted from it. I've heard from countless men and women unable to find love. Knowing that there were so many single and searching women out there looking for a man like me gave me hope and reminded me that I lived in a world of endless options. I've heard from numerous men and women who are too afraid to approach someone they found attractive because they don't want to look desperate, creepy, or make someone uncomfortable. This helped me realize that most men don't have the testicles to talk to women or men they want and most women don't have the ovaries to do it either. Therefore, all I needed to do was find my testicles and I'd be the exception. And I've heard from countless couples in unhappy, unhealthy, dysfunctional relationships. Hearing what's gone wrong in their lives helped me to realize how to avoid making the same mistakes in my own relationships. Whether it's a man looking for a woman, a woman looking for a man, a man looking for a man, or a woman looking for a woman, there's a common thread that ties us all together—none of us is taught how dating and relationships work. We're just supposed to figure it out on our own. I can tell you with absolute certainty, I figured it out.

Now, it's your turn.

The five steps in this book unfolded over a lifetime of personal and professional relationship research spanning over thirty years. It was only as a single and searching twentysomething man living in Chicago that I spotted trends, patterns, and an undeniable secret truth at the root of it all. Unlike Carrie Bradshaw in *Sex and the City,* a lot of my time was spent having a lot of no sex in the city. While I did experience an occasional hookup, date, and relationship, my love life was mostly the product of a series of fortunate accidents. I just wanted to find a girl who could love me as much as I loved her.

The answers started to surface when I began writing my Help Me, Harlan! advice column in my college newspaper. A year and a half after launching the column, I was reaching millions of readers in dozens of local daily and college newspapers, including the New York *Daily News,* where I shared a page with Ann Landers. People would reveal their darkest secrets and most perverted problems (my favorites). I'd reach out to experts to help research and shape my answers and ensure that I was being responsible, thoughtful, and not completely full of bullshit. After years of in-depth research, thousands of letters answered, and a personal dating experiment during which I put into practice what I'd observed—I found the love of my life and the answer to the questions everyone has been asking me for the past seventeen years. This book is the answer. . . .

BEFORE STEP 1 . . .

Welcome to the beginning of this book and the end of the drama.

Do me a favor and start reading this in a place with a lot of people. I'll give you time to get somewhere busy (a coffee shop, restaurant, bookstore, park, food court, airport, train station, busy street, house of worship, etc.). Make sure you do this during the day and while totally sober (or within the legal driving limit).

Once you arrive, stand up. Seriously, take a good look around. If you're reading this on an airplane, wait until the seat belt sign is turned off. If you're reading this in church or at temple, wait until the congregation is asked to rise. If you're reading this in a movie theater, it must not be a very good movie.

Survey the area. Look for someone attractive or cute enough. You do this all the time. It should be easy. Find someone? No? Keep looking. If you can't find anyone or can't find a busy place to look for people, go to an online dating site or do some Facebook creepin' and look for someone who catches your eye.

QUESTION: When you see someone who gives you *that* feeling, what do you do? Do you *always* approach that person and start a conversation? Or do you mostly wait, stand, stare, and hope that someone else will say or do something?

THE ANSWER: Most people will do nothing. And most of the time nothing will happen. Sometimes someone else will do something, but then if that someone isn't anything special we're left with nothing.

NEXT QUESTION: What if you knew with absolute certainty that, at all times, you had thousands of people who wanted to hook up with you, have sex with you, and do everything you wanted to do in a consensual way? Would you ever hook up or sleep with someone who might be in a relationship, married, lying, or hiding a secret sex souvenir that will make you itch or burn when the sex ends?

THE ANSWER: No, not likely (at least while sober). Yet, millions of people hook up with people they barely know, allow themselves to be used, use others, get hurt, itch, burn, and have regrets after the hookup and sex ends.

NEXT QUESTION: If you knew that, at all times, you had thousands of people who wanted to date you, love you, and treat you the way you deserve to be treated, would you ever put up with one person who treated you like shit, didn't return texts, ignored calls, humiliated you in public or in private, verbally abused you, hit you, or treated you any less than the way you deserved to be treated?

THE ANSWER: NEVER.

NEXT QUESTION: So, why do so many people put up with so much crap, stay in bad relationships, make excuses for inexcusable partners, and run back to exes they should be running from?

THE ANSWER: We learn from the earliest age that dating isn't about options, it's about accidents. It's not about exploring opportunities to find love, but avoiding opportunities to get rejected and feel bad about ourselves. As a result, being in a bad relationship can be better than being in no relationship.

LAST QUESTION: What if you knew that at all times you lived in a world of endless options, could take emotional risks at will, and knew that you could find sex, love, and passion simply by embracing a secret truth, getting comfortable in your thongs (I'll explain that part later), and always expressing what you felt regardless of how vulnerable it made you feel?

THE ANSWER: By the end of this book, this will be your reality. You'll have the emotional stamina to take risks at will. Your world will be one filled with endless opportunities to find love, lust, or whatever you desire. Where you once saw opportunities to get hurt, you'll find new opportunities to find happiness. You'll look at friends, strangers, dating, relationships, and what it means to be in love differently. Most important, you'll look at yourself in a whole new light.

When you do find love (and you will), if things go badly, instead of making excuses for a relationship that's flawed you'll fix it or find something better. You won't get caught up in games, hide your feelings, or be consumed with what he or she is thinking. You'll have the ability to express yourself freely and listen without apprehension. You will have the courage to demand and command respect. You will have the confidence to find endless partners who are "just that into you." You will not hesitate to commit. You'll no longer worry about settling. The process in which you meet people and build relationships will not allow for it. You will find more than just a date, you will find happiness in love, and in life.

One more thing—I promise not to waste your time. I guarantee this book will help. It might take a few days, weeks, months, or even years, but I promise, it *will* happen. And when it does happen, you'll know why and how it happened. And knowing how you found love and happiness means that should you lose it, should it ever end, or should it not work out as planned (it happens), you will know how to find it again and again.

THREE PROMISES

◆ **CAUTION:** The five steps in this book will work, but for them to be guaranteed to work, you first must make three promises to yourself. Without making these promises, you will just set yourself up for more drama and disappointment. You must commit to do the following three things.

PROMISE #1

You *must* believe there is more than one person in the world who will want you.

◆ **Warning:** When you meet someone using these five steps (and you will) and that person sexts you after the first date, you'll need to move on to the next option. Unless you know that you have options, you'll convince yourself that receiving a picture of a penis is kind of sweet. (Note: Some of you might be into this, but before or after a first date is not the right time.)

PROMISE #2

You *must* believe you're worth dating.

◆ **Warning:** When you meet someone using these five steps (and you will), if you don't think you're worth dating, you'll hang on to the first person who wants you because you won't think anyone else will. And should that person start treating you like shit you'll think, "Could be worse. At least I'm not alone."

PROMISE #3

You *must* believe this approach will work for you.

◆ **Warning:** Using the five steps in this book will be uncomfortable at times. You might even want to vomit. If you're not occasionally uncomfortable you're doing something terribly wrong (or you're just drunk). It will be extremely easy to give up. You must have a burning desire to make this work. Be a skeptic, but be a positive skeptic who is willing to commit to change, and this will change your life.

PART I

Why We Think Men Are Assholes,
Women Are Bitches,
and Couples in Love Suck

Our Informal Relationship Education

We learn to read. We learn to write. But no one teaches us how to find a date or how to find the love of our life. It's all just *supposed* to happen.

We flirt on Facebook, secretly stare at our crushes, and wait for IT to happen. We go to school dances, hang out, hook up, date, fall in love, and break up. When it all ends, we have no idea where, when, or how it all happened. In the meantime we are bombarded with images, status updates, and articles about love, lust, and getting lucky. Even sixteen-year-olds are getting pregnant on reality television while we're longing for love. We look for guidance, but there isn't much out there. Most parents don't know how it happened or are still struggling to find answers. Friends who find themselves in relationships don't know how it happened. And porn sites don't exactly offer a lot of practical dating advice.

BEST DATING ADVICE #620–#625

#620. *Never date someone you can't see without makeup on.*
—from a best friend

#621. *Quit beating yourself up and being such a dumbass.*
—from a father

#622. *I never received dating advice. I'm gay and live in a homophobic town.*
—from no one

#623. *If you're willing to let his penis inside you, you should be able to talk to him.*
—from a friend

> **#624.** *Don't make a boy your everything; when he's gone, you're left with nothing.*
>
> —*from a sister*
>
> **#625.** *Be genuine from the very beginning. It is a waste of your time to win over someone who isn't going to like who you really are.*
>
> —*from my parents*

We spend years receiving a formal education so we can go find a career that feeds our passion, but little time learning how to find passion in our relationships. Some of us move on to college to get a more formal education. It's during the college years we learn that we don't need to know anything about how to find love to hook up or fall in love. All we need is beer, a buzz (alcohol speeds up the process), and to spend a lot of time in rooms with a lot of people. Dating isn't about exploring options; rather, it's about fortunate accidents. It's a game of luck and hoping something sticks. And this is when it all gets sticky. It's a lot of trial and error, but after a few tries most of us don't have the emotional stamina to continue. That's when we hate, hide, give up looking, hope it happens when we least expect it, or settle for the least offensive option until something better comes along.

When we look back at what went wrong, there are five lessons we learn during our informal education that set the stage for drama and confusion.

My biggest fear is being hurt, used, or rejected. It has made me less likely to try dating or talking to guys I'm interested in. It makes it difficult to have the courage to approach someone and talk to them.

—Kirsten, nineteen, single

We Learn . . .
Sharing Our Feelings Is Stupid
(or Just a Very Bad Idea)

It all starts with a first crush. That's when we first smell danger. It's also when we first learn that sharing our feelings is a VERY BAD idea or just plain stupid. From the first "like" our knee-jerk reaction is to avoid letting anyone know. We might confide in a friend or two, but the only way we are willing to openly share our feelings is if we are 100 percent certain the person we like will like us back.

We'll flirt, ask friends to ask questions, creep on Facebook, ogle, Google, and investigate, but rarely say what we feel. We get as much information as possible without letting the people we like know we like them. We want to know if someone is available and interested. We ask friends to do our dirty work for us. The reason we use friends is so we can distance ourselves far enough to deny our feelings ever existed should the person we like not reciprocate or others find out about them. Technology and friends give us a safe buffer to cast blame and run like hell should rejection or humiliation find us.

As a result, we have imaginary relationships with people who don't know they're in relationships with us (thank you, Facebook). We get jealous of people who like the people we secretly like. We have friends find out information about the people we like, which inadvertently gets the people we like interested in our friends because they are the only ones talking. Most friends won't date the people we like, but some will. It's difficult not to blame them. It's hard to meet people.

If we do share our feelings and our crush shares our interest we breathe a sigh of relief. If a crush doesn't share our feelings the results can be devastating. It only reaffirms why it was wrong and stupid for us to share our feelings in the first place. We quickly learn that sharing our feelings and not having them reciprocated is about the worst thing that can happen. We can't stand the pain of not being liked by the people we like. If other people find out it's that much more humiliating. So we learn to hide our feelings and run like hell when we smell rejection coming.

Step 1 will give you the power to say and do what you feel without the fear of being rejected and/or humiliated.

> My biggest hang-up was me. I was so worried about how I was perceived by other people that I didn't get involved. It was self-preservation.
>
> —*Heidi, twenty-six, married*

We Learn . . . We Are All Defective

When a crush doesn't want us, we think: It's me. I'm ugly, unattractive, and not good enough. No one will want me. I'm defective. And why do we think this? It's what we're told. It's what we tell ourselves. It's what we hear other people saying about the people we watch share their feelings and get crushed. We forget the undeniable fact that not everyone we like will always like us. We just see rejection as meaning we are defective. It's all we're equipped to think at first. Some of us never change that self-destructive thinking.

If you want to listen to people say horrible things to one another, hang out in a junior high school cafeteria. Teenagers can be mean (understatement of the book). Twelve- and thirteen-year-olds are some of the most dangerous of the human species. Adjectives like "desperate," "disgusting," "stupid," "slutty," "flat," "fat," "short," "stinky," "horny," "ugly," "creepy," and all other horrible words that tear people down are part of regular conversations among friends. And I understand why it happens. It's hard to be comfortable in your own skin when you're a prepube with raging hormones and hair sprouting from random places. The goal is to make everyone feel like less so we can feel like more, only everyone ends up feeling like less. And it sets us all up to feel defective when it comes to the world of dating and relationships.

Rejection is hard enough to handle at any age, but rejection in a world where everyone already feels so uncomfortable makes it unbearable. No one wants to be reminded that he or she isn't good enough. So to avoid feeling defective, we learn it's safer, smarter, and easier to keep our feelings a secret—that is, unless we're approached by someone who wants us or we know with absolute certainty that someone we want won't reject us. Then we can consider letting down our guard and being vulnerable.

What's wild is that we can feel completely defective, hate sharing our feelings, and still find love (or just hook up). Feeling defective and being in an intimate relationship can be a dangerous combination. It's hard to demand and command respect when you're not sure anyone else will want you. It's easier to make excuses for people who treat us poorly, take back partners who treat us like crap, and hang on to flings that should have been flung. It's impossible to see that we have options when we are just so grateful that someone could love someone as defective as we might be. We learn that to be with anyone means to be rescued from the land of the single and searching.

Step 2 will help make you feel good enough and hot enough—always.

I met a guy I liked, and we watched movies at his place. We hooked up, and then I left because we both had class the next morning. The next day I wanted to see him again. He said that he wanted to talk to me about something. This is when he made it clear that he wanted to keep hooking up, but he didn't want to date me. He said there was a certain type of girl he wanted to date, girls he had "known awhile and hadn't done anything with." I asked if that meant I was exempt from the list just because of the night before, to which he said, "Well no. I wouldn't have dated you anyway."

—Ashley, nineteen, single

We Learn . . . Hooking Up Is Faster and Easier Than Dating

Put yourself in a room with other people long enough and you'll hook up. Put yourself in a room with alcohol and it will happen faster (not recommended).

We soon learn that while we can be totally unable to share our feelings and not feel attractive enough, we can still hook up. This describes most high school relationships. We learn that hooking up is a lot faster and easier than dating. It's much more efficient because sharing feelings and expectations is not required. Plus, you know you aren't defective if someone is hooking up with you (post-hookup is a different story). Hooking up can happen with a random stranger or someone we've known and secretly wanted for months (or years). Instead of sharing our feelings while sober and clothed, we make excuses about why we shouldn't, telling ourselves we don't want to lose a friendship, make things weird, or make people uncomfortable. But then, if the night is right and drinks are flowing, we suddenly forget to make excuses and hook up with the people we've secretly wanted, but have been too afraid to tell. We learn that the hookup can be a perfectly "safe" way to connect—but it can also lead to drama and disaster.

Some people use hooking up for fun (a hookup can range from

a kiss to all-out sex). Others use it to start relationships. Not knowing what will happen post-hookup can lead to excitement, drama,
or disappointment. When the hookup ends, it can get weird *fast*.
Clothed and confused, we have most of the same questions we had
before the hookup, but now it's all heightened because everyone
got naked—and that makes it harder to have an honest conversation: *Should I call? Should I text? Does he like me? Will she call me?
Did she like it? Was I good? Will it happen again? Am I annoying?
Am I in love? Did we use a condom? How could I let this happen? I'm
so stupid. . . .*

The confusing part of hooking up is that it can lead to happy
and healthy relationships. It can also lead to drama and devastating
disappointment. People who are great at hooking up can be terrible
at sharing their feelings and feel completely defective. Sharing feelings and feeling good enough is not required before, during, or
after the hookup. And that's why it's easier and faster than dating.

Step 3 will force you to stop making excuses and help you make
dating as easy as, if not easier than, hooking up.

17 FORMS OF THE COLLEGE HOOKUP

1. **The Drunk Hookup:** an alcohol-induced connection
2. **The Friendly Hookup:** friends who go way beyond friendly
3. **The Rebound Hookup:** broken up and looking for some Band-Aid lovin'
4. **The Cheating Hookup:** no dignity here
5. **The Desperation Hookup:** looking for anyone—and I mean *anyone*
6. **The Online Hookup:** a high-speed connection
7. **The Who's Next Hookup:** the love junkie who can't get enough
8. **The Ex Hookup:** reliable, dependable, and oh so easy
9. **The Visitor Hookup:** here today, gone tomorrow (aka the hit and run)
10. **The I Love You Hookup:** love at first sight (until the morning light)
11. **The Convenience Hookup:** the closest person with a pulse gets some
12. **The First Week Hookup:** action exclusive to welcome week
13. **The I Just Want to Have Fun Hookup:** it's all good fun until someone falls in love
14. **The Weekend Hookup:** I love you Friday, I love you Saturday, but don't call me Sunday
15. **The Sympathy Hookup:** a charitable donation (it's always generous to give)
16. **The Help Me Hookup:** hooking up with a teaching assistant, resident assistant, or inappropriate helper
17. **The Repeat Backup Hookup:** a go-to guy or girl who is the backup love buddy (aka the 3:00 A.M. text message booty call)

Source: *The Naked Roommate: And 107 Other Issues You Might Run Into in College*

We Learn . . . We Don't Know Where, When, or How It Happens (But Still, It Happens)

We quickly learn that hooking up, dating, or finding love is unpredictable. We don't need to know where, when, or how it happens, but still, it happens. There's a reason it's called getting lucky.

The random nature of it all adds to the excitement at first, and later, to the anxiety. We can hang out, hook up, date, get married, have kids, share intimate moments, and still never know how we got there. And this is where it gets confusing.

Not knowing where, when, or how it happens means not knowing if it will happen again. And not knowing if it will happen again means being more inclined to hang on to whatever we have—even if it's not that good. When we find something better, we question what we already have. We either ignore our feelings, talk about them, or cheat and talk about them later—after everything blows up.

Because we learn that dating and hooking up is random and unpredictable, we have a hard time seeing that we have other options. As a result, too many people stay in bad relationships too long, make excuses for inexcusable behavior, and stick with partners who they should run from.

* * *

Step 4 will give you the power to make it happen again and again and know how the hell it all happens.

> I met my husband on spring break. I wasn't even looking for a husband. I had one serious relationship prior so I think I knew what love felt like. We both knew early on that we were in love. We got married a year and a half after meeting and honestly we are both very lucky that we fell in love with someone who was a good match. We've been married for thirteen years and have gone through a lot, but feel we have a great marriage—again we are just really lucky. He makes me laugh every day.
>
> *—Jen, thirty-seven, married*

We Learn . . . Men Are Assholes, Women Are Bitches, and Couples in Love Suck

We eventually learn that most of our crushes, hookups, and relationships won't end in marriage—just hurt feelings.

When we get hurt we think, He's an asshole, She's a bitch, and Couples in love suck. Or we just hate ourselves. Our survival instincts kick in. Rejection hurts. It's our worst fears confirmed. Someone we like (or love) doesn't want us. It reaffirms what we already knew—sharing our feelings is stupid or we're too defective to be loved. If we've been cheated on or betrayed, we can't help but wonder what we did wrong.

The knee-jerk reaction when someone hurts us is to become a hater or a hider. We hate because anyone who hurts us is the enemy. We want to make them hurt as much as they've hurt us. We hide because seeing that person is too painful. It can be like looking in a mirror and facing our insecurities. We don't want to look. It's just too sad and humiliating.

If we're the ones doing the rejecting, we become the assholes and bitches. No one wants to be the bad guy (or girl) and see the pain we've caused. So, instead of being honest, we text our feelings, ignore people who like us until they go away, or just cheat and wait until it all blows up. When it finally ends we're even bigger assholes and bitches than had we shared the truth earlier.

Having tasted love and not being able to find it again can make us bitter. Never finding it in the first place can fill us with resentment. And then, we see couples in love, couples that are far less attractive, a lot less interesting, and not nearly as successful. We see friends getting engaged, getting married, and starting a life together when we're still looking to find a decent date. While the people we look at with envy might not be any happier than us, we can't help feeling more alone and discouraged than ever.

STEP 5 will give you the power to never settle and to handle whatever comes your way.

GETTING NAKED TIP #431

Want to avoid being treated like shit? When someone treats you like shit the first time tell that person, "You can't treat me like shit." Then explain what bothers you. The second time it happens simply say, "I told you, I don't like being treated like shit. Good-bye."

A total loss of contact is the most hurtful thing a woman has done to me. Giving a reason I can understand, but leaving unanswered questions can really suck. The human mind can be a real jerk in these situations because one is likely to think of all the times that they might have done something wrong. I know that is what I do, and I also know I am not alone.

—Grant, twenty-one, single

Despite What We "Learn"

Despite what we learn during our informal relationship education we can still hook up, find a date, have sex, get married, and have a family. All it takes is hanging out in rooms, a few drinks, and a ring. We can be horrible at sharing our feelings and never feel good enough, yet we can still find someone to love and someone to love us. We can have no idea how it happens, but can still experience deep intimacy. We can hate being single, dread time alone, and still fall in love. Sometimes a relationship will work. Other times it won't. When it doesn't work, what went wrong can be traced back to either our informal relationship education or our partner's informal relationship education.

The five steps in this book are what we *should* have learned. It's a way to look at dating, relationships, and hooking up that could have cleared up the confusion and saved a lot of time and tears. Finding love doesn't have to be so difficult. It doesn't have to be so emotionally grueling. It's just how we've been taught to make it.

And now, that's all about to change. . . .

PART II

<·····················>

The Getting Naked Experiment: 5 Steps to Finding the Love of Your Life (While Fully Clothed & Totally Sober)

Introduction: The Getting Naked Experiment

TIME TO GET NAKED

The time has come.

Your Getting Naked Experiment is about to begin. Your job is simple—follow the five steps in this section and you will be able to say what you feel, do what you've always wanted to do, and find the love of your life, and more. As you conduct your experiment, ask yourself the question, "What have I done today to change my current situation?" If you're in a relationship, ask yourself, "What have I done today to make my situation better?" Do nothing, expect nothing to change. Do something, expect everything to change.

NAKED ADVICE

Dear Harlan,
Where are all the good guys hiding? I'm told I'm an
attractive girl, but I can't seem to find one. Suggestions?
   Searching

Dear Searching,

They're everywhere.

    The problem is that most of them don't have the testicles to approach you. And most women don't have the ovaries to approach guys who interest them. Every time you see a man who catches your eye, use your big ovaries and let him know that you're interested. Then see if he can find his testicles and talk to you. Just to be clear—I'm not suggesting you literally whip out your ovaries and he take out his testicles; it's a metaphor.

The Getting Naked Experiment

Welcome. It's time to undo the damage.

Imagine you are taking a class in which your final exam is an experiment that requires you to take risks so that you can find a date, hook up, or fix a problem in your current relationship. Your grade depends on satisfying several criteria. If you're single, you must conduct a Getting Naked Experiment during which you'll commit to approaching people and being approached by people who catch your eye. You'll identify people YOU want to date and either ask them out or get them to ask you out (if you're old-fashioned). If you don't want to date, you may choose to conduct a Naked Hooking Up Experiment (no sex, just kissing), but you must hook up with intention and purpose. This means you must know how the hookup happened and what you did to make it happen. You must understand what happened so you can make it happen again and again. Hookups by way of fortunate accidents do not count. If you're already in a relationship, you can conduct a Naked Relationship Experiment. This means facing uncomfortable issues that you need to address within your current relationship.

Sex is not part of your Getting Naked Experiment, but expect that people you meet will want to have sex with you. If you choose to have sex (feel free to wait), you will be required to know the person's first and last name (and how to spell it, just in case you need to find them later). You must know if your partner is single or married and if he or she has any sexual souvenirs (herpes, HPV, chlamydia, etc.) before sleeping together. And finally, you must be comfortable enough to talk about what having sex means to you, your partner, and the relationship BEFORE having it (i.e., are you now committed and monogamous?). If you are conducting a Naked Hooking Up Experiment and choose to have hookup sex, you must address all the same questions (this will help you avoid drama, itching, and burning). If you are conducting a Naked Relationship Experiment, expect more frequent and better sex once you work through uncomfortable issues, assuming you're still together.

The final part of the assignment: This all has to be done while sober. No, don't close the book! You *can* have a drink or two (depending on your weight, what you ate, and how much you ate before drinking). Getting Naked means staying under the legal driving limit (typically under a .08 BAC). Totally sober is ideal, but if your driving isn't legally impaired, your judgment shouldn't be. Bottom line: You can have a glass of wine, just don't get drunk.

To complete your Getting Naked Experiment, you will need to abandon everything you've learned about dating and relationships up to this point in your life. Start fresh and leave old thinking behind. I know this isn't entirely possible, but please try. This will be a life-changing experiment. The world is your petri dish. Once you fully commit to Getting Naked, you'll be ready to begin the process and take the first step.

* * *

◆ **Note to Readers:** For more information on the three different experiments, turn to Part Three: The Getting Naked Experiment and visit www.gettingnakedexperiment.com.

NAKED ADVICE ··············▶

> *Dear Harlan,*
> *I'm interested in a guy, but can't tell if that guy is interested in me. How can I tell?*
> *Interested*

> *Dear Interested,*
> *Hmmmmmmmm. Ask him.*
> *Nah. Just wait until your twenty-five-year high school reunion and tell him you had a secret crush on him. Then he can talk about the secret crush he had on you. Then you can meet each other's spouses.*

Embrace the Secret Truth

MEET THE UNSPOKEN AND UNDENIABLE TRUTH

[Fill in your name here], meet the unspoken and undeniable Truth.

The Truth is that thousands of people will want you and millions will not. This is called The Universal Rejection Truth of Dating and Relationships and it's one of the most powerful and undeniable truths in the universe. It's a truth that's started wars, ended marriages, and caused countless people to get drunk out of their minds for centuries.

THE UNIVERSAL REJECTION TRUTH OF DATING AND RELATIONSHIPS (The URT)

NOT everyone you want will want you. Thousands will, but millions will not.

No matter how much or how little you have, how attractive or unattractive you might feel, how smart or funny you might be, not everyone you want will want you. Thousands of people will want to hold you, kiss you, and spread love oils on you; millions will not. We love it when people love us, but we hate it when they don't. In fact, it's painful. We don't just think it's painful; research has proven that rejection feels the same as a physical punch.

> Along with a team of colleagues, Smith found that intense emotional pain can activate the same neural pathways as physical pain. So being rejected can really hurt in a visceral, physical way as if you've really been punched.
>
> —Time *magazine, April 11, 2011*

Rejection isn't painful because we are weak. It's painful because it hurts. It's how we are hardwired. When we feel like we are getting hit in the gut, it's really as if we're getting hit in the gut. No wonder we will do whatever we can to avoid it. But this creates a huge obstacle because finding love means having to take risks that might lead to rejection. This means, in order to take the risks needed to find love (while sober and clothed), we *must* be able to handle the possible pain of rejection before, during, and after a relationship. For peace-loving people, the idea of physically hurting someone or getting hurt seems wrong, but rejection is part of the normal and natural process of finding love.

We're told that dating is a numbers game, but few of us are equipped to take the number of risks needed to find it. Most of us don't have the emotional stamina to handle the people who won't want us. We can only handle being punched in the gut so many times before we get damaged, desperate, or give up. The undeniable fact is that some people will want us and many more will not. The more we can focus on all the people who want us, the less everyone else matters.

You have a choice: fight The Truth or accept The Truth. If you choose to fight The Truth, you might want to stop reading and use this book to balance a wobbly table—at least then it will be useful for you.

◆ **Note to Readers:** The Universal Rejection Truth of Dating and Relationships may be referred to as The URT at times in this book.

NAKED ADVICE · · · · · · · · · · · · · ➤

Dear Harlan,
I hate men. I finally told my longtime crush that I was interested in him and he told me he likes my best friend. What do I do?
    Pushed Aside

Dear Pushed Aside,
Tell him he's a horrible person for telling you the truth. Then explain that when you like a guy, he has to like you or he's a big asshole. When you're finished calling him names, explain that you didn't mean what you just said. You were hurt and have a hard time handling rejection. Then ask if he will still be your friend because anyone who can be this

honest with you is someone you want to keep in your life. If
you're afraid of looking a little unstable, avoid calling him
names and accept that not everyone you want will always
want you, regardless of how hot you might be.

MOST HURTFUL THING SOMEONE HAS SAID OR DONE #448

Her ex-boyfriend was visiting her over the weekend from
another city. She told me, her current boyfriend, it would
be best if I didn't come around.

EMBRACE THE TRUTH

Being aware of The Universal Rejection Truth of Dating and Relationships and embracing it are two very different things. It's the
difference between being aware of deodorant and applying it. If
you don't apply it, you'll stink. Not embracing The Universal Rejection Truth of Dating and Relationships will cause you to reject
rejection and stink at dating and relationships.

> There is a difference between knowing the path and
> walking the path.
>
> —*Morpheus to Neo, from* The Matrix

After writing my column for the past seventeen years, answering thousands of letters, visiting hundreds of college campuses, and talking to thousands of people, I can tell you with absolute certainty that most of the world is unaware of The URT or unable to embrace it. Not embracing The Truth is called being in a state of rejection denial.

Rejection denial is a dark and dangerous place where you think everyone you want should want you. Meaning, if I like you, you must like me. If you don't like me, I will hate you or hide from you. In fact, I might even draw a hate circle around you and hate everyone who likes you. I might get my friends to hate you and hide from you. We will possibly spread rumors, attack you, or stalk you. I'm *that* unwilling to give you permission to think anything other than what I want you to think.

Irrational thinking? Yes. Totally. Completely.

Fighting The URT is a losing battle. It can't be beat. Rejecting rejection will just create more rejection and make you miserable. It will consume you. Rejection is as normal and natural as breathing. Fighting The Universal Rejection Truth of Dating and Relationships will lead you to blame yourself or everyone else for not giving you what you want. The blame turns into resentment and the resentment becomes bitterness. Then you end up giving up or settling for whatever you can find or what finds you. Accepting The Universal Rejection Truth means accepting that when you face rejection, the problem isn't always you or the people not giving you want you want—it can be The URT. The five steps in this book will help you make this distinction.

We are all imperfect. Dating is imperfect. Embracing our

imperfections is what makes us perfect and what makes dating tolerable (or even fun).

Make this the moment you recognize that The Universal Rejection Truth of Dating and Relationships exists. Appreciate that thousands of people will want you and millions will not. Give the ones who don't want you permission to think whatever they want without hating, hiding, or feeling humiliated. Give the ones who will want you access to you. The more you focus on the end result (finding love and happiness) the sooner you will find what you desire.

NAKED ADVICE ·············▶

Dear Harlan,
Do you believe that we all have one soul mate? I have a
hard time believing there is only one person who is my soul
partner.
    Soul Searching

Dear Soul Searching,
ABSOLUTELY!
    And conveniently, most soul mates live down the block,
sit next to us in class, or work in the next cubicle. Unfortu-
nately for you, your one and only lives in Tikka Tikka
(a small town in Eastern Nigeria).
    Actually, I don't believe we all have only one soul mate.
I believe we have a lot of them. Some soul mates are better
than others. Some are in our lives to teach us lessons and

then move on. Others stay in our lives forever. Once you know you have more than one, you can find the best one and get rid of the soul mates that treat you like crap. And should you bump into other soul mates later in life, you don't have to dump the one you're with. You can acknowledge the other soul mate and think, "Ah, another one." Then love the one you're with.

THOUSANDS OF PEOPLE WILL WANT YOU

This is the page where you acknowledge that thousands of people want you (this is a very good part of the book). At this moment, there are thousands of people who think you are attractive, intriguing, intelligent, interesting, and hot. They are waiting to meet you. This might be hard for you to appreciate—especially if you're reading this on a Saturday night sitting alone with a big burrito (that's not slang, I'm literally talking about a big burrito). Up to now, your world has most likely been very small. When you run and hide from The Universal Rejection Truth of Dating and Relationships this happens. In the past, you were more focused on avoiding getting hurt than finding happiness. As a result, you haven't been able to see all the people waiting and wanting to love you. There are literally thousands of people at this very second who want to hold you, touch you, and spread love oils on you. They are eager, longing, and hoping to meet you. Never forget this.

Don't believe you have options? Can't find your 1 in 311,341,249 in the United States? Then relocate to China. Spend time in rooms with 1,336,718,015 Chinese people and you will get lucky. Hang out in Bangkok in the red-light district and it will happen even faster (not recommended). If you strike out in China, try India (1,189,172,906 people). If India doesn't work, use your miles and head to a beach and finish this book. **Steps 2** through **5** will change this way of thinking.

◆ **Note:** If you meet a billion people and you can't find someone, the problem might be you. No worries. **Step 2** will fix this.

Of course, some of us have more options than others. Bisexual readers have the most (congrats, bisexual readers, way to go!). Heterosexual singles have the second-most options (you still have plenty, no worries). Gay and lesbian singles have the third most (relax, you still have plenty of options, it just takes more work to find people who are out and available or in the closet and eager to come out to be with you).

Still can't believe you have options?

Browse any popular (or unpopular) online dating site and look through the profiles. You'll find millions of people out there. Some are people you know. Most are strangers. And then there are the millions of singles who don't make themselves available online. When you're done thinking about this, consider people in relationships who will soon be single. It's hard to see all the options because most people don't walk around advertising their relationship statuses (except maybe on Facebook).

We live in a world with thousands of options. From the office to the classroom, from the gym to the coffee shop, from a walk around the block to a trip across the country, there are people who will want you. They are waiting online, waiting to go on blind dates, at church, at temple, in airports, at concerts, at parties, at bars, in parks, on trains, on planes, on buses, in elevators, and everywhere else you live, work, and play. We are surrounded by endless opportunities to meet people who will want us. The moment you accept and embrace that you live in a world with thousands of options is the moment your world will begin to get bigger, brighter, and better.

NAKED ADVICE ············▶

Dear Harlan,
I recently started college and I'm suddenly finding that guys are looking at me differently. This didn't happen to me in high school. I was from a small school and was never the most popular or prettiest girl. I don't know how to react to the attention. I've never even been on a real date. I don't want to disappoint anyone with my lack of experience so I just avoid the people who like me. Any advice?
   Suddenly Wanted

Dear Suddenly Wanted,
Running will only make you hotter, especially on a hot and humid summer day. Admit it. You're hot. Don't get embarrassed. Come out of hot denial and give yourself permission to be wanted. Hot denial can be an ugly place where you can't admit you're attractive and deserve to be

loved. The biggest risk is that when you do finally connect
with a man, you allow him to treat you like crap, because
deep down, that's what you think you deserve. Men who
judge you because you aren't experienced are the big losers.
Teaching a hot inexperienced girl how to love and be loved
can be hot—even hotter than running on a hot humid
summer day.

GIVE THOUSANDS OF PEOPLE PERMISSION TO WANT YOU

Once you can begin to acknowledge that there are thousands of
people in the world who will want you, you'll need to give these
people permission to want you. This might sound simple, but having only started embracing The Universal Rejection Truth a few
pages ago, it can be more difficult than you think.

The problem with giving people permission to want you is that
you might not want all of them. And if you don't want someone,
you'll have to do the rejecting (this is called being the rejecter). We
all know how much rejection hurts. Again, peace-loving people
don't like hurting other people. It can be hard to hurt someone. So
it's easier to avoid everyone. When you avoid everyone you make
it harder for someone to approach you. And that's not fair to you
or him or her. Being honest with people you're not interested in
dating is not called being cruel. It's called being honest (rejection by text or rejection by silence is cruel). Think of it as freeing

someone up so he or she can find someone else who can appreciate his or her best qualities. If people who like you can't give you permission to reject them, recognize that they are in rejection denial and give them this book. Highlight and dog-ear this page.

REJECTION BY SILENCE

Ignoring and avoiding people who like you and hoping they will go away.

Giving people permission to want you is also difficult because it means being vulnerable and opening yourself up to possible hurt. When someone you like also likes you, it feels ohhh so good. You might connect emotionally and physically. If sex is involved, there's even more at stake. As time passes, this person might decide he or she no longer wants to be with you. Now, someone you know on an intimate level is rejecting you. And that can really suck. It can be even more painful.

Once you complete **Step 2** you'll be able to minimize the pain. And once you complete the rest of the steps it will be far easier to move on and give more people permission to want you. At this point, giving people permission to find you hot might be too hard for you. Don't worry—it will get easier with each passing page.

NAKED ADVICE · · · · · · · · · · · · ·➤

Dear Harlan,
I'm in high school and have a serious crush. I want to let a
guy in choir know I'm interested in him, but if he's not
interested I'll be ruined. I can't avoid him because we are
in choir together. What should I do?
  Crushing

Dear Crushing,
If you can't handle him NOT wanting you, you're not ready
for him to want you. Here's the problem—if he likes you, your
relationship will be about trying to keep him interested in
you. That's when good girls get into trouble (drinking, drugs,
16 and Pregnant). Make sure you can give him permission to
not want you before giving him an opportunity to want you.
Otherwise, you'll risk losing yourself, the guy, and the choir.

MILLIONS OF PEOPLE WILL *NOT* WANT YOU

If thousands will want you, millions will not. There's no easy way
for me to put it—not everyone you want will want you. No matter
how much or how little you have, how big or how small it is, how
funny or how smart you are, NOT everyone will want you.

You can be hot, hilarious, and extremely well hung and you'll get rejected. You can be beautiful, brilliant, and have a perfect body and you'll get rejected (thank you, reality dating shows). Smile, rejection is something we all have in common. People you know will not always want you. Strangers you meet will not always want you. It doesn't mean you're defective. It doesn't mean you need to change. It's just The Universal Rejection Truth of Dating and Relationships.

Rejection isn't about being defective. It's about one person choosing one good thing over another good thing. If you don't think you're a good thing, **Step 2** will help you start to feel like a very good thing. For now, all you need to do is acknowledge that not everyone you want will always want you.

Some people will NOT want you because you're the wrong race, religion, sexual orientation, or ethnicity. Some people will NOT want you because they are married, engaged, or going through a divorce. Some will NOT want you because they are emotionally unavailable or think you're out of their league. Some will NOT want you because they have a sex souvenir (herpes, HPV, HIV), are pregnant, or are dealing with personal issues that leave no time for dating.

Also, appreciate that there will be people who don't want you because they are not physically attracted to you. You might be too tall, too short, too blond, too brunette, too red, too skinny, too fat, too hairy, too bald, too small, too big, too good-looking, or too *something* that makes you NOT attractive to someone.

◆ **Note:** Turn back to the previous pages if you need a reminder of the thousands who will want you.

And then there will be people who will NOT want you because of your personality, lifestyle, or character. You might be too funny, too serious, too confident, too shy, too rich, too poor, too drunk, too sober, too boring, too boisterous, too self-centered, too outgoing, too driven, too lazy, too dishonest, too righteous, too corrupt, too pure, too motivated, too distracted, too kind, too mean, too loving, too nurturing, or too uncaring.

No matter what you say, no matter what you do, no matter how fit, strong, or successful you are in life—not everyone you want will always want you. And likewise, not everyone who wants you will always get you. There's only one of you and billions of them. Rejection and oxygen are two things we all have in common. Breathe deep. There's no avoiding either.

NAKED ADVICE · · · · · · · · · · · · ·➤

Dear Harlan,
I told a guy I've liked for a while that I have feelings for him. And then he told me he has a girlfriend. I'm so humiliated. I don't know how to look at him again. What can I do to help with the damage control?
  In Hiding

Dear In Hiding,
What damage? Someone got to him before you. When he's done dating her, he can try to date you. If you're dating someone when he approaches you, tell him you have a boyfriend. When you break up with the other guy you can see if this guy is single. If he's not, wait until the timing

works. One day, it will work (or it won't). But if you're busy feeling humiliated, you'll hide and it will never work. Give him permission to be hot and unavailable, but don't let it humiliate you. Now he knows you like him—that's a good thing.

MOST HURTFUL THING SOMEONE HAS SAID OR DONE #446

My boyfriend was dating my friend and me at the same time . . . and neither of us knew it.

GIVE MILLIONS OF PEOPLE PERMISSION TO NOT WANT YOU

Knowing that some people you want will not want you isn't the same as giving these people permission to not want you. It's like getting breast implants and expecting everyone to love them. Not everyone will love your new DDD cups (too big). Giving people permission to think whatever they want means that you respect their choices, even if you aren't their first choice. It means NOT hating and NOT hiding from them because they don't want to date or sleep with you.

The moment you give people permission to be authentic and think whatever *they* want to think is the moment you become free to think whatever you want. It's when you get back all the power. The goal is no longer, WANT ME! LIKE ME! THINK ONLY GOOD THINGS ABOUT ME! It's more, WHAT DO I WANT? WHAT DO I LIKE? WHAT DO I THINK ABOUT YOU? Remember, you are giving people an opportunity to be with you. If someone doesn't want you or can't recognize your best qualities, then move on. Focus on the thousands of people who will want you.

Being comfortable in the face of rejection makes you far more attractive and interesting to people who will not want you. It's not that you're cocky or arrogant—it's just that you know you have options and have embraced The Universal Rejection Truth of Dating and Relationships. The fact that you're not humiliated by one person's rejection can change how that person sees you. It can rattle him or her. Some people will get angry because you're not upset enough. Some might think you're playing games. Some might suddenly find you more intriguing. While it might appear that you don't care, the truth is you do care, but you've given someone permission to not want you. You don't care to spend more time thinking about it. When you know that you have options and can embrace The URT you know that rejection doesn't mean you're defective. Your reaction to people not wanting you makes you appear self-assured. And that's attractive. There's a reason that so many relationships start with rejection. Sometimes it takes people time to realize that you're the very best option. What matters most is that you know it.

The challenge isn't giving one person permission to not want you, it's giving a lot of people permission. After enough rejection, even the most comfortable people can start to question themselves and lose hope. **Step 2** will address this. For now, start to give people permission to think whatever they want. Soon, you'll have the emotional stamina to handle it all.

NAKED ADVICE · · · · · · · · · · · ·➤

Dear Harlan,
My boyfriend doesn't like me to do anything other than
hang out with him. He gives me a guilt trip whenever I tell
him I want to hang out with my friends. Help!
   Suffocating

Dear Suffocating,
Know why your boyfriend doesn't want you to hang out in
rooms with other people? He's afraid you'll find someone
better. He doesn't want to get hurt. Know what? He's right.
He knows himself much better than you do. Good boy-
friends don't isolate, control, and get jealous when their
girlfriends have other friends and occasionally go out with
them. Just the wildly insecure bad ones do.

GETTING NAKED FACT #540

Meet people during daylight hours. It's easier to see someone's personality (and looks) during daylight hours. Plus,
people tend to be sober during the day (unless it's Mardi
Gras or you're at a tailgate party).

PUT YOURSELF IN MORE ROOMS

It ALL happens in rooms. People who work together, go to school together, and make movies together hook up, date, and fall in love. Rooms aren't just places with four walls. They can be indoor and outdoor spaces where people have shared experiences over a period of time. They can be classrooms, chat rooms, ballrooms, workrooms, coffee shops, parks, playing fields, pools, beaches, trains, planes, gyms, bars, clubs, dances, singles' parties, etc. Once you embrace The Universal Rejection Truth of Dating and Relationships, you'll find it easier to put yourself in more rooms with more people. The more rooms you hang out in, the better the chances you'll find a date, hook up, and fall in love.

Embracing The URT makes it easier to put yourself in more rooms because you will give people in those rooms permission to think whatever they want. Once you're around more people, you'll get to know them. Instead of focusing on what they are thinking about you, your focus turns to what you think about them. It's the difference between eating alone and assuming everyone thinks you're a hungry loser versus eating alone and thinking about all the people you can sit with the next time you are eating alone.

If you always find yourself in the same rooms with the same people, change your routine. Eat in different rooms, sit in different locations, work out at different times, work on new projects that will help you meet new people, attend classes at a different location, and go out on the weekends (even if you're tired) so you can put yourself in more rooms. If you want to meet other single people, put yourself in the same rooms with single people who identify themselves as single and searching. Do your meeting during the day. Plan times to get together at night. Online dating sites, speed-dating events, and singles' parties are just some of the places where single people identify themselves while hanging out in rooms. Have friends set you up so you can be in more rooms with more single people. Once you embrace The Universal Rejection Truth, train in your thong (**Step 2**), stop making excuses (**Step 3**), and take risks (**Step 4**), you will have the testicles or ovaries to talk to people in rooms at will and find the love of your life (**Step 5**). Getting lucky won't be about blind luck or accidents. It will be about intention, purpose, and putting yourself in the path of opportunity—or in a lot of rooms with people (while clothed and sober).

NAKED ADVICE ·············➤

Dear Harlan,
I'm terrible at making conversation. I never know what to say. Any suggestions for how I could be better at making conversation?
   Bad Talker

Dear Bad Talker,
Are you listening to me? I know you don't listen to other people. I'm worried you're not listening. Hello! DO YOU HEAR ME?
   Here's the problem—it's impossible to be a good talker unless you're a good listener. Once you start giving people

permission to think whatever they're going to think and know you're good enough to date, instead of thinking about all the bad things they're thinking, you can actually listen to them. Then you can think of something to say. If you never listen you will never be a good talker.

Hear what I'm saying?

BEST GETTING NAKED APPROACH #703

Comment about the scenery, a book, or something happening in the moment. It's less shocking and embarrassing than focusing on me. The worst is saying something purely physical that just says you're looking for a piece of ass. You may be, but don't come right off with it.

BEST GETTING NAKED APPROACH #704

Say something nerdy, but not too dirty. Examples: "I had to talk to you, you pulled me in like a black hole" or "If I cook dinner, will you bring a 3.1415 . . ."

BEST GETTING NAKED APPROACH #705

"Hi, how are you, I'm _____, what's your name?" is a much better way to start. Women respond better when a man seems like he's interested in who they are, instead of just seeming like he wants to take them home with him.

TALK TO PEOPLE IN ROOMS

Once you embrace The Universal Rejection Truth of Dating and Relationships, conversation will come more easily. You can start talking to people in rooms without worrying about saying the wrong thing. If you're terrible at making conversation, don't worry, that will change by **Step 4**.

Until now, talking and listening has been hard. When you're consumed with what everyone is thinking, it's impossible to hear what they are saying. The voice inside your head overpowers the real conversation. It's all about, *Does he like me? Does she like me? Do I look creepy? Why is he looking around? Why is she checking her phone? Is she annoyed? Does my breath smell? How do I look? Is there something in my teeth? Should I ask him out?* When it's your turn to speak you don't have much to say because you haven't been listening. You've been pretending to listen. Instead of having a conversation, it's more like reading a script or conducting an interview. Eventually you run out of questions and the interview ends. Half of talking is listening. It's the more important half. Embracing The Universal Rejection Truth will quiet your mind and help you become a better listener and talker. And embracing The URT will make it much easier to do it sober (or mostly sober). Why? The more a person drinks the less that person cares what other people think. The alcohol quiets the mind. Embracing The URT has a similar effect. Once you give people permission to think whatever they want, you don't have to get drunk to open your mouth and quiet your mind.

The next big question—what's the best way to initiate a conversation? Hello. I actually mean "hello." Dirty, suggestive, and crude might work on some people, but most people will not be impressed when you ask, "Is that a mirror in your pants? Because I see myself inside them." Saying hello can be a much bigger turn-on. Once you've embraced The Universal Rejection Truth of Dating and Relationships, you'll find that you can be surprisingly interesting and engaging.

Step 1 will help you find the courage to talk to people in rooms. **Steps 2, 3, 4,** and **5** will keep you talking.

◆ **Worth Noting:** Never assume someone is not interested in you until you know. He or she might just be too busy thinking about what you're thinking.

NAKED ADVICE • • • • • • • • • • • • ▶

Dear Harlan,
I've been hooking up with a good friend and have fallen for her. We promised we wouldn't get emotionally involved. It was only going to be sex. Now, I want something more committed, but I'm afraid this could ruin the friendship. Do you have any suggestions about how to approach this?
    Friend with Benefits

Dear Friends with Benefits,
How about dinner before sex? Then before dessert, make it clear that you care about her too much to have a purely sexual relationship. Give her permission to just want sex,

but be prepared to stop having sex with her. Sleeping with her makes you emotionally unavailable for anyone else. Should you keep sleeping with her and then find a girl-friend, your friendship with her will end. You can't stay friends with a booty call and be in a serious relationship. Not cool. Either you two are platonic friends or a couple. The benefits have run out.

REGRETTABLE SEXUAL MOMENT #113

I went home with a guy and my friend went home with his roommate. We had a good time hanging out and then we took it to his bedroom. Mid-thrust he states, "I have a girlfriend!" and then starts crying. Come to find out his girlfriend was one of my friend's little sisters. I felt abso-lutely terrible. But in hindsight I had no idea they were dating.

DATE OR HOOK UP WITH PEOPLE IN ROOMS

Accept The Universal Rejection Truth of Dating and Relationships and you'll have the power to hook up or date people in rooms with-out feeling like it's all one big fortunate accident. It will be done with clear intent and purpose.

DEFINITION: THE HOOKUP

A hookup can be anything from a kiss to all-out sex. A Naked hookup as defined in The Naked Hook Up Experiment is simply a kiss—not sex.

The more time you spend talking to people in rooms, the better the chances you'll get lucky. Getting lucky can mean a date, a kiss, lust, love, or a connection that can lead to something in the future. Up to now, hooking up has been the easiest and fastest way to connect. The problem is that post-hookup, it's hard to know if someone likes you or just likes hooking up with you. Sometimes a hookup can turn into a relationship, but a lot of times it doesn't.

Once you've embraced The Truth, you can know how the hookup happens. More important, you will know it can happen again and again. And knowing how it happens and that it will happen again means having more control. You can choose to hook up first and date later or date first and hook up later. You now have options.

You can take time to see if you like someone before having sex. You can take time to see if someone likes you before having sex. When sex isn't about validation or getting someone to like you, there's no urgency. Once you fully embrace The URT (and complete **Step 2**), sex doesn't need to be used to win people over or to feel desired. It can be something you do with someone you like, or love. It can be about connecting on a deeper level. It's easy to like having sex; it's harder to like someone you have sex with.

Once hooking up and dating aren't random luck you can do it with intention. You can control how far and fast you go and what happens after you get naked. Post-hookup, you'll have more power and less regret. You can talk to people you've hooked up with and not worry about ruining anything. If someone wants to hook up with you again or date you, that person needs to talk to you and treat you a certain way. If not, you know you have options and you can move forward.

In the past, too many questions meant possibly ruining an opportunity to get lucky. Now, it means respecting yourself enough to find out what you're getting into or what's getting into you—not so much to ask.

NAKED ADVICE ·············➤

Dear Harlan,
My boyfriend never introduces me to his friends as his girlfriend. We are exclusive, but he doesn't tell anyone. What's up with this?
    Secret Girlfriend

Dear Secret Girlfriend,
I've got a secret for you—YOU HAVE A TERRIBLE BOY-FRIEND! Either he has another girlfriend, is embarrassed to have you as a girlfriend, or is too afraid of what his

friends are thinking. None of this is respectful. If he can't introduce you as his girlfriend you can introduce yourself as his new ex-girlfriend.

BIGGEST MISTAKES SINGLE FRIENDS MAKE #317

They NEVER let go, no matter how miserable they are with a person. The thought of being alone is somehow much worse than picking up the pieces and moving on. If there's more pain than pleasure, it's not worth it.

DEMAND RESPECT IN AND OUT OF ROOMS

When you embrace The Universal Rejection Truth of Dating and Relationships and know you have options, it will become easier to avoid assholes, bitches, and anyone who treats you poorly. When someone treats you poorly once, you can stop it before it happens again. If it happens again, you move on and never look back. Remember the question from page xvi:

QUESTION: If you knew that, at all times, you had thousands of people who wanted to date you, love you, and treat you the way you deserved to be treated, would you ever put up with someone who treated you like shit, didn't return texts, ignored calls, humiliated you in public or private, verbally abused you, hit you, or treated you any less than the way you deserved to be treated?

ANSWER: NEVER

The reason we get in the habit of putting up with cheaters, abusers, and bad partners is because most of the world hasn't embraced The Truth, doesn't feel hot enough to find someone better, and forgets (or doesn't know) there are options. Demanding respect means honestly sharing our feelings. Honestly sharing feelings means possibly driving someone away and ending up single. Ending up single is the last thing someone in rejection denial wants. Losing someone when you don't know how you found that person can be devastating—especially for someone so insecure.

The moment you fully embrace The Universal Rejection Truth of Dating and Relationships and know you have options is the moment you will begin to demand and command respect. If someone doesn't want to listen to you or acknowledge your feelings, you now have the power to leave the relationship and find someone who will respect you. You can do it faster, with more confidence, and without regret. That's the power of living in a world of options and not fearing The Truth.

Dear Harlan,
I've been dating a guy for a couple of years, but I'm not
sure if he's the one. He's employed and I love him, but I'm
not sure if I need more excitement. He's talking about
getting married. I can't tell if he's the one or if I'm settling
for him because he can give me everything I need. I want to
be crazy for him, but I'm not so sure. Help!
   Indecisive

Dear Indecisive,
Ignore your gut. Marry your employed man. Hope that
things get more exciting (maybe he'll get a promotion). If
it doesn't, have some kids to make things more exciting.
If that doesn't work, have an affair. When you get
caught, and the marriage begins to crumble, go to couples
therapy. Following the divorce, make sure you find
someone with a more exciting job the second time
around. OR you can avoid the marriage, kids, affair, and
divorce by finding something more exciting now. Work on
making it more exciting now. If it doesn't get better, go
to premarital counseling. But don't fool yourself into
thinking it will get better by doing nothing and ignoring
your gut. Nope. It won't.

MOST HURTFUL THING SOMEONE HAS SAID OR DONE #447

A guy lied to me about not breaking up with his other girlfriend. When I asked him about it, he got really mad at me. Literally screaming at me, scaring the shit out of me. It got to the point where I had to beg him for forgiveness for even asking if he was dating another girl (he was actually seeing two at the time). Yeah. Doesn't make much sense to me either.

WELCOME TO A BIGGER, BRIGHTER, AND MORE FORGIVING WORLD

It's like flipping a switch. In an instant, you begin to see the world and everyone around you in an entirely different light. When you accept and embrace The Universal Rejection Truth of Dating and Relationships and know that you always have options, the world becomes brighter, bigger, and much more forgiving.

Dating and relationships is no longer about avoiding pain, but rather, pursuing passion. You no longer fear taking risks. You recognize the endless opportunities all around you. It's easier to be happy. One person can no longer destroy you. You no longer have to hate or hide from people who don't give you what you want. You are in control of how it all goes down (or most of it). Life is more about what YOU want instead of wanting to be wanted.

You no longer need to feel trapped in bad relationships. You don't need to make excuses for inexcusable partners. You don't have to put up with cheaters or become one. Once you stop trying to control what people think, you can listen to what *you* think and hear what others are saying. You don't have to try as hard to win people over. You don't need to be validated by people who want to use or discard you. People can like you or not. Dating isn't about getting married—it's about having a good time and sharing interesting experiences. It's about learning what you love and don't love. It's more fun and less drama.

STEP 1 CONCLUSION

Step 1 is now complete. Take a break. Walk around. Grab a snack. Go for a run. Do yoga. Do whatever you do to relax, but don't begin your Getting Naked Experiment quite yet. You must read **Step 2** before you begin. I know you might feel motivated and ready to find love (or lust), but unless you complete **Step 2** (and the rest of the steps), you'll risk taking one step forward and three steps back.

Here's a quick recap of **Step 1** before moving on to **Step 2**:

◆ There's a secret, unspoken, and unavoidable truth called The Universal Rejection Truth of Dating and Relationships. The Truth says that not everyone you want will want you. Thousands will, but millions will not.

◆ Most of the world is stuck in a state of rejection denial. Once out of denial, you can give people permission to think freely without hating or hiding from people who don't give you what you want.

◆ You have thousands of options. In order to see the options, you must give people permission to want you.

◆ Not everyone you want will want you. Embrace it. Don't fight it. Rejecting rejection just causes more rejection. Accept The Truth and focus on the people you want to meet, date, and love.

◆ Once you embrace The URT, you can put yourself in more rooms, talk to more people in rooms, hook up with or date people in more rooms, and demand respect from people you meet in rooms.

◆ Once you embrace The URT, you'll see opportunities to take risks and find love where you once only saw opportunities to get hurt. Your world will be bigger, brighter, and much more forgiving.

Train in Your Thong(s)

INTRO TO TRAINING

Welcome to **Step 2.**

For this step you'll need to bring an open mind and three pairs of thong underwear (yes, men too). One will be for your body, one for your head, and one for everything else (it will all make perfect sense in a few pages). Your thong wearing will be done in private. If you're uncomfortable with the idea of wearing a thong, you can imagine wearing a thong (but wearing is strongly recommended). If you don't have a thong and can't get your hands on one fast enough, you can always use this page (after you read it).

Dear Harlan,
I'm not the most well endowed. I know this. I always get anxious when it comes to the moment of truth. I don't want to disappoint a woman with my lack of size. How can I not let this be the thing to hold me up?
   Small

Dear Small,

Don't be so quick to think you're so small. In some coun-
tries you might be large. In some lighting you might be
huge. In some situations you might be enormous—a virgin
might not have much to compare you to. But I'll be honest,
some women like a bigger man. That said, a man who can
provide engaging conversation, a delicious dinner, a
sensual back rub, mind-blowing oral sex, and passionate
lovemaking only to end the night by cleaning and vacuum-
ing the apartment can make a girl reevaluate the impor-
tance of a bigger package. In other words, use what you've
got and then clean up.

TRAINING IN YOUR THONG

The thought of taking a risk and meeting people who may or may
not want you might make you want to vomit. I'll give you a moment.

(a private moment for you)

Step 1 gets you inside rooms. **Step 2** will help you build the
emotional stamina needed to stay inside them. To get the results
you desire from your Getting Naked Experiment, you must get
comfortable being vulnerable. Forget being vulnerable in front of
other people. **Step 2** is about being vulnerable while completely
alone, in a room, in front of a mirror, while wearing a tight thong
(yes, thong underwear). Before you can let anyone see you in your

tight thong, you need to get comfortable with the uncomfortable. Otherwise, you'll be too busy turning off the lights, running, and hiding from the insecurities hanging out of your thong.

Think of dating and relationships like the sport of boxing. Boxing involves standing in the ring and getting beat up at times. Taking a physical and emotional beating is an unavoidable part of the sport. While no one should be punching anyone while dating (light biting and spanking may be acceptable), dating can be painful at times. Research has proven that the brain interprets getting rejected the same way it does taking a punch. So, in a way, boxing and dating are connected. You can dislike getting hit and do everything possible to avoid it, but if you want to find the love of your life, you need to be willing to take the emotional punches while taking emotional risks and meeting people. Otherwise, you'll get knocked out.

Remember, there will be thousands of people who will want you, but there will be millions who will not. Yes, millions. Until you've trained in your thongs, you will keep missing out on all the people who will want you because you'll be too busy protecting yourself from all the people who won't.

You need to train in order to have the emotional stamina needed to find the thousands of people waiting to meet you.

Dear Harlan,
*My girlfriend makes me turn out the lights when we have sex.
I like to watch. But she says it makes her feel self-conscious.
I find this strange considering we are having sex. It doesn't
get more vulnerable or intimate than that. Help?*
    In the Dark

Dear In the Dark,
*You can always be less obvious—try introducing can-
dles into your lovemaking (beware of the hot wax), try
using night-lights (do it near outlets), and try using the
natural lighting of the moon (do it outdoors). Still, it
would be nice if you could turn on the lights without
turning her off. Try using your other senses to help her get
a better sense of self. Start with your ears and listen to her
fears and concerns. Then use your mouth to remind her
that you understand and love all of her. Then follow up
with a touch. Make her most uncomfortable spots the
most attractive. If you smell trouble—stop. The more ways
you can communicate that you love all her parts, the
easier it will be for her to forget to turn off the lights and
get turned on.*

GETTING NAKED FACT #912

In 1960, the median age of a first marriage for men was 22.8 and 20.3 for women. In 2010, the median age of a first marriage for men was 28.2 and 26.1 for women. Translation, there are more single people than ever.

Source: U.S. Bureau of the Census, www.census.gov

WHY A TIGHT THONG?

Training is about being vulnerable. There are few pieces of clothing that make us feel more vulnerable and exposed than a tight thong. Even being naked can be less vulnerable than standing in a room while wearing a tight thong. Naked can at least be liberating. A thong just makes stuff hang out.

Step 2 is about looking in the mirror while wearing your tight thong and knowing that no matter what's hanging out, it's worth loving. It's about knowing you are hot and desirable at all times. If you can't love what's hanging out of your thong, at the very least you'll need to learn to accept and tolerate it or you'll never feel comfortable allowing anyone else to see you in or out of your thong. You'll be too focused on what you're lacking instead of what you have. Remember, it doesn't take training to find someone willing to take off your thong. It just takes being in a room. It's possible to find love (or lust) and be uncomfortable in your thongs. But that's not Getting Naked.

In the past, you've been able to cover up the things hanging out of your thongs by using random hookups, bad relationships, alcohol, drugs, excuses, excess, booty calls, serial relationships, and poor lighting. There's no more running or hiding from the beautiful, ugly, and shocking truth. The time has come to turn on all the lights and let it all hang out.

NAKED ADVICE · · · · · · · · · · · · ▶

Dear Harlan,

I've been dating a guy who opens doors, buys me flowers, and compliments me. He's nice. In fact, he's TOO nice. And I don't know why I have a problem with it. In the past, I've dated guys with bad reputations and suffered the consequences. I don't want to break up because someone is too nice, but it just feels wrong. What the hell is wrong with me?

    Nice Girl

Dear Nice Girl,

Good news—there is no shortage of men who will treat you like crap. Before throwing a good one away, experiment with being respected. See if you can find excitement without being treated like crap. Tell him things you've never told anyone. Share your deepest insecurities. Be vulnerable to the point of being scared. Go on adventures. Get the thrills you used to get from the chase by creating new challenges—healthier ones. Also, consider finding a therapist. The problem might be connected to your relationships with the men in your life—like a dad who neglected you. Should you want to be treated poorly, try role-playing. You can be the naughty bad girl, and he can discipline you.

THE NAKED PEOPLE IN YOUR CORNER

As you conduct your Getting Naked Experiment, you'll get knocked around. This is to be expected. At times you'll question yourself and what you're doing. You'll forget you're attractive, interesting, and dynamic. You'll need people to turn to. You'll need advice, guidance, and support. You'll need people to tell you the things you **want** to hear and the things you **need** to hear. You'll need people to remind you that you're attractive when you feel ugly, smart when you feel stupid, and desirable when you feel anything but. You'll also need people to tell you when your pants are too tight or when you need to keep your pants on.

Some of you have the wrong people in your corner—rotten, toxic, bad people who take pleasure in seeing you get hurt. Some of them are aware of what they're doing. Some are clueless. Like a boxer who enters the ring, you need to have people in your corner who want you to win. If the people in your corner want you to lose, you will lose. Some of you have people in your corner who are threatened by your success and secretly like it when you get knocked down. It makes them feel better. Get away from them.

Make sure you respect and trust the people in your corner. They will need to tell you the truth. You'll need them to be brutally honest. You must give them permission to tell you not just what you want to hear, but what you need to hear. This can be painful, humiliating, and hard to hear. Call it tough love (or no bullshit). You must trust their intentions. You must feel safe with them in your most vulnerable state or you will shut down and push them away. You must value their opinions and trust their sensibility.

Some of these people should be family and friends. You should also have professionals, such as psychologists, psychiatrists, counselors, therapists, doctors, surgeons, dieticians, nutritionists, and trainers. As you conduct your Getting Naked Experiment, you will keep adding and subtracting people. Some people will be better than others in different situations. The more comfortable you get in all of your thongs, the easier it will be to identify the right people who can help you find what you want.

One last thing: YOU are the most important person in your corner. No more beating yourself up. No more telling yourself horrible things about you. You must be your best friend, not your worst enemy. Be kind to you.

◆ **Note:** If a new boyfriend or girlfriend is threatened by the people in your corner—BEWARE! It's a sign your partner wants to control you—the fewer people you have in your corner, the easier it is for someone to control, use, or abuse you.

NAKED ADVICE · · · · · · · · · · · · ➤

Dear Harlan,
My friends hate my boyfriend. He's made a few mistakes in
the past (he cheated on me once) and really hurt me. But
he says he's changing his ways. What can I do to convince
them he's not a bad guy? He's my first real love and I'm not
ready to lose him.
Unfriendly Friends

Dear Unfriendly,
Maybe he can date all your friends or cheat on you with
them—then everyone can understand how great he is!
When your closest friends hate your boyfriend, it's because
he's easy to hate. Either you can't see it or don't want to see
it. Maybe seeing it would mean being single. Any woman
who lets a man treat her like this can't have very much
self-confidence. Unless he's been in therapy and can tell
you exactly why and what will be different this time
around, you're just bullshitting yourself. Fortunately, you
have friends in your corner willing to tell you the truth.

WHY YOU MUST TRAIN PHYSICALLY

Can I talk about your boobs?

No? Well, I'm going to anyway. I don't know you, but I'm guessing you either have big boobs, average boobs, small boobs, perky boobs, hard-to-find boobs, saggy boobs, uneven boobs, boobs with big nipples, boobs with small nipples, boobs with three nipples, boobs with stretch marks, boobs with birthmarks, boobs with freckles, boobs with a hair on top, soft boobs, firm boobs, one boob, no boobs, fake boobs, young boobs, old boobs, or middle-aged boobs. Getting a little creeped out that I'm talking about your boobs? I give you permission. But trust me, I'm going somewhere with your boobs in the next paragraph.

I promise you with 100 percent certainty that no matter what kind of boobs you have—thousands of men (and women) will love to get close to you and your boobs (look around and see all the men and women who like boobs furiously nodding). If you're happy with your boobs, substitute whatever body part makes you uncomfortable and you'll find thousands of people who will love that, too. Not everyone will love it all, but training in your physical thong means giving people permission to love it or leave it. Cellulite, blemishes, birthmarks, you name it—we can look beyond it all.

No matter how big, small, tall, short, bald, hairy, bent, or protruding—people will love what you hate. That is, unless you don't or can't learn to love it. Then it will define and destroy you. You will convince yourself that whatever is hanging out of your thong is the reason you're single or not wanted. You'll think you're defective.

You'll believe everyone else is better. You'll be unable to take risks because getting close to someone will just mean getting hurt.

Training in a thong is critical. You need to know at all times that you're good enough or hot enough. You need to know that rejection isn't about being defective. It's about a person choosing one good thing over another good thing. But unless you think you are a good thing, you'll think you're nothing. That's when we get desperate, jealous, hold back, make excuses, lie to ourselves, lie to others, hate, or hide. Training will change this.

Remember, you can be in a room long enough, hook up, and find love without ever being comfortable in your thong. It doesn't mean the love will last. Couples who are uncomfortable in their thongs and fall in love can easily end up questioning their relationships, controlling each other, and living in the dark—that is, until one day they face the truth and realize it's not working. Save yourself the time and get comfortable in your physical thong now.

NAKED ADVICE · · · · · · · · · · · · ➤

Dear Harlan,
I noticed in your photo that your ears protrude. I think you would be far more handsome if you had your ears surgically pinned back. Have you ever thought about having surgery? If so, I think you would be much more attractive with flatter ears and find more success with women.
    Donna from Dallas

Dear Donna from Dallas,

Thanks, I hear ya. While I always appreciate a friendly suggestion to get my ears surgically stitched closer to my head to not look as ugly, I'm not sure I agree with you. At one point in my life, I might have agreed. I even contemplated getting them fixed, but then realized nothing was broken. My ears weren't the problem. It was how I saw them. I soon came to the realization that my ears separated me from all the flat-eared men of the world. They are fun to play with and hold on to. They are erotic toys. Women who don't want me because of my ears don't interest me. My ears are a small part of me that I've learned to love. Besides, if I changed my ears, I'd look like everyone else. And I like looking like me.

GETTING NAKED FACT #915

You must know that you are hot and desirable at all times. If not, you'll feel ugly and undesirable. And that's just not attractive.

HOW TO TRAIN IN YOUR PHYSICAL THONG

It's time to grab your training thong and find a private space . . .

A Training Guide

1. Find a room with a full-length mirror and a door that locks.
2. Walk inside the room, close the door. Lock the door behind you.
3. Turn on all the lights (you'll want to see everything).
4. Slip on your tight thong (nothing else).
5. Look at yourself in the mirror from top to bottom.
6. Acknowledge the parts of you that you love. It could be your smile, hair, body shape, body size, or big toe. If you think you have NO good qualities, jump ahead to the next paragraph. Whatever you love about yourself, embrace it. Embracing it means appreciating that no matter how someone responds to you in your thong, these qualities can never be taken away. These are your best qualities. Some people will love them, others will not. If your gift is a big toe, focus on the people who have foot fetishes. That's accepting and embracing what's in your thong.
7. Next, acknowledge the parts you don't like hanging out of your thong. Start with your head and scan down to your toes. Keep a running list of your imperfections. These are the things you love to hate. Acknowledge them. As painful and uncomfortable as it might be to look at them, don't turn away. Once you finish your thong self-exam, feel free to cover up.
8. Commit to changing what you don't love.
9. Commit to loving what you can't change.

Your choices are simple. Acknowledge what's hanging out of your thong, or reject and deny what's hanging out of your thong. If you choose to reject and deny, make this the last page of the book you read until you seek professional help. If you're ready to accept what's hanging out of your thong, please continue reading.

NAKED ADVICE · · · · · · · · · · · · ▶

Dear Harlan,
I want to get my boobs done. I want them fixed. I'm lacking in the chest and have always felt self-conscious, especially at the beach and in the locker room. I don't want to be big, just comfortable. I don't see a problem with this, but my parents strongly disagree with my decision. Thoughts?
  Boobless

Dear Boobless,
You have broken boobs?
*   If you feel bigger boobs are a fundamental part of your femininity, then carefully consider expanding your bust. Yes, some men (and women) enjoy bigger boobs, but speaking on behalf of most men, we like a variety of boobs. Really, no boob is a bad boob. And a flatter chest can have its perks. People look you in the eyes, back pain is minimal, and you don't have to worry about sagging. Fix how you see your chest before fixing your boobs. Understand exactly why you want bigger boobs and how a bigger bust*

will change your life. As for your parents, they probably see a beautiful girl who wants elective surgery—it's hard to blame them for discouraging it.

WHY YOU MUST TRAIN EMOTIONALLY

Can I talk about all of your issues?

No? Well, I'm going to do it anyway. I don't know you, but I'm guessing you have secrets. We all do. You might be sad, happy, rich, poor, struggling, shy, boring, passionate, bipolar, bisexual, bi-winning, lesbian, homosexual, heterosexual, autistic, attention starved, distracted, depressed, divorced, recently diagnosed, healing, hurting, dateless, sexless, a survivor of sexual abuse, pregnant, expecting, cheating, grieving, codependent, dependent on drugs, on probation, on meds, a victim, a survivor, a child of privilege, a child of divorce, an orphan, a child of a single parent, self-conscious, overly ambitious, underemployed, lonely, in the midst of a crisis, or in a state of bliss and no one can understand why you're so damn happy (I want some).

I promise you with 100 percent certainty that no matter what issue(s) you're dealing with, thousands of men or women will love getting close to you and the issues hanging out of your thong. They will love how in touch you are with yourself and find you courageous and intriguing. Your ability to embrace your imperfections will provide one more reason to find you attractive and worth dating. In fact, it will make it easier for the people you date to be open and honest about the issues hanging out of their thongs.

The problem isn't that you have issues—it's that you've let them define you and stand in your way. Until you train emotionally, these fears, insecurities, and secrets will hold you back and make you think that you are not good enough. You will be too worried to say what you feel and express yourself. You will hate or hide because facing them will be too painful.

To be intimate, you need to be vulnerable. To be vulnerable, you need to train in your emotional thong.

NAKED ADVICE · · · · · · · · · · · · ➤

Dear Harlan,
I'm told that I'm an attractive girl, but I've only been on a couple of dates. I feel like something is wrong with me. My friends have all been in relationships and I'm still single. I'm starting to lose hope.
   Hope Fading

Dear Hope Fading,
I'll share a secret with you—you could be scary attractive. Most guys just will not approach an attractive girl while sober. They wait until it's safe. They wait until they know you are interested. Or they wait too long. Your friends might be better at making it safe for guys to approach them or may not be as attractive. Want to find a relationship? Make it as easy as possible for guys to ask you out or do the asking. Can't do it? Figure out why taking a risk is so scary. If you

*think you're attractive, interesting, and someone worth
dating, it shouldn't be a problem. Maybe you don't really
think you're attractive, interesting, and worth dating.
Could that be the problem? Don't let being single make you
think you're not good enough—you could be too good.*

HOW TO TRAIN IN YOUR EMOTIONAL THONG

It's now time to grab your next training thong and find a private
space. . . .

Training Emotionally

1. Find room with a full-length mirror and a door that locks.
2. Walk inside the room, close the door. Lock the door behind you.
3. Place a clean thong on your head. (Note: you don't actually
   need to put it on your head. It's more of a metaphor.)
4. Look at yourself in the mirror.
5. Begin by focusing on your best parts. Focus on your
   kindness, personality, charisma, optimism, intellect, mo-
   tivation, ambition, resilience, boldness, authenticity, self-
   lessness, tenacity, and other amazing assets. Never forget
   these qualities. No one can take these away from you. If
   you find that you have NO good qualities, stick with me.
6. Now focus on what makes you uncomfortable. What
   are your secrets? Why don't you feel good enough? What

happened? How have you been hurt? Why are you in a bad relationship? Why do you hate men or women? Why do you blame others for your misfortune? Why can't you move forward? Why don't you deserve the best? Why do you overeat? Why do you make yourself vomit? Why do you starve yourself? Why do you have unprotected sex? Why do you need to drink so much? Why do you do drugs? Why is it so hard to be authentic? Why are you obsessed with what everyone thinks? What do you hate about being alone? What happened in your past that still haunts you? Why can't you trust people? Why can't you commit? Why do you constantly seek approval from friends, family, or strangers? Once you finish looking at yourself and conducting your emotional thong exam, take a break and clear your mind.

7. Acknowledge the best and worst parts of you that are hanging out of your thong. Acknowledge them and embrace them. As painful and uncomfortable as it might be to see them, don't look away.

8. Commit to changing what you don't love.

9. Commit to loving what you can't change.

Your choices are simple. Accept what's hanging out of your thong, or reject and deny what's hanging out of your thong. If you choose to reject and deny, make this the last page of the book until you seek professional help.

If you're ready to acknowledge and accept what's hanging out of your thong, please continue reading.

NAKED ADVICE ·············▶

Dear Harlan,
I hooked up with a guy I met last night. I don't want to be
annoying, but he said he would text me the next day and
hasn't. I want to text him, but I don't want to bother him
or seem overeager. How long should I wait?
   Waiting Game

Dear Waiting Game,
Wait until about 3:00 A.M., just after last call, when he's
looking for some action. If he's not hooking up with
someone else, you might get a quick response. As a rule—if
you're too afraid to text after a hookup, that's not someone
you should be hooking up with again. Text him if you want
to talk to him. Give him a chance to respect you or reject
you. If he doesn't text back, move on. A man who wants to
see you again will text you back.

Bonus Advice to Guys: Women want attention, not games. If you
like someone, don't make that person wait. If a girl you like doesn't
like attention, she's not worth your attention.

WHY YOU MUST TRAIN SPIRITUALLY

To find the love of your life, you must have faith. Having faith means trusting there are thousands of people who want you without seeing them standing in a line in front of you. It's believing with unwavering certainty these people will appreciate and desire you and what's hanging out of your thong(s). It means trusting you will get what you want, even when it seems furthest away. It means expecting you'll get hurt at times, but knowing you will heal and move forward. Having faith is believing and knowing, no matter what, that it can and it will happen.

Training in your spiritual thong means always taking care of you. It means asking yourself the question: Should you ever lose someone you love, what would you have left? If the answer is NOTHING, you must train spiritually. You must possess passions, interests, and qualities independent of a significant other. You must have relationships that no one can take from you (this can include a relationship with G-d, friends, and family). You need to have the ability to spend time doing the things you love to do with you.

Training spiritually means establishing a loving and trusting relationship with you. If you have nothing more than the person you're dating, you will be nothing without someone.

Most important, training spiritually means having the unrelenting faith to believe that no matter what happens, you will always be okay. We are resilient. We are survivors. We are stronger than we know. With proper training, the right people in your corner, and the ability to accept and embrace The Universal Rejection Truth of Dating and Relationships, you will get what you desire.

To find the love of your life, you must have faith.

Dear Harlan,
I have a hard time believing I live in a world of thousands of options. I find that the best men are either gay or already taken. How can I believe there are all these people out there who will want me when I'm having a hard time finding one?
Losing the Faith

Dear Losing the Faith,
I could tell you about the millions of people who are single and searching, show you pictures of people who are far less attractive than you who found love, or take you out on a date (that one might hurt my marriage), but I still wouldn't be able to convince you that you live in a world of options. It's bigger than me or someone else convincing you. It's like believing in a G-d or trusting your food is being prepared by someone with clean hands—it's faith. The only thing you can control is how you feel about yourself. The more centered, balanced, healthier, happier, and more attractive you feel while not being with the love of your life, the easier it will be to have faith that you will find him.

HOW TO TRAIN IN YOUR SPIRITUAL THONG

Training spiritually doesn't involve putting on another actual
thong (phew). It's about looking inside yourself and being completely vulnerable while together with you.

Training Spiritually

1. Make an appointment with yourself. Find a time and
   space with no distractions where you can be with you.
2. Ask yourself one question: What have I experienced in
   my lifetime independent of romantic relationships that's
   given my life meaning? Include hobbies, interests, personal,
   professional, or athletic accomplishments and experiences.
3. Ask yourself one more question: What do I want to experience in the future independent of romantic relationships
   that will give my life deeper meaning?
4. Visualize doing these things. Imagine what it will feel
   like doing these things. Commit to doing one of these
   things.
5. Put together a plan on how you can do this one thing.
6. Turn to people in your corner to help you plan how to do
   this one thing.
7. Create and commit to a time line for doing this one thing.
8. Repeat the process and do one more thing.
9. Continue doing more things for the rest of your life.

Training spiritually means creating a life you love independent of a romantic relationship. It's feeding your soul and finding a space in the world that belongs to you. It's finding ways to express yourself that no one can stop you from doing. Do things that give you pleasure and you will always have something to do, a place to go, and ways to find balance. Having interests outside of a relationship will also make you much more interesting when in a relationship. It means not having to depend on your partner to be the only thing that gives your life meaning. The more you enjoy spending time with you, the more other people will want to spend time with you.

Explore new interests. Dive deeper into old ones. Challenge yourself physically, emotionally, or intellectually. Take a wine-tasting class. Learn how to give a massage. Run. Hike. Study religion. Meditate. Try yoga. Teach. Paint. Start a movement. Volunteer. Travel. Get a part-time job doing something completely ridiculous just because you want to and can. You don't even have to tell anyone. Just start by doing one thing. Once you get a taste, you'll hunger for more. Soon, you'll find yourself doing things you love in rooms with people who love doing the same things. And we all know what happens when you spend time in rooms with people. . . .

NAKED ADVICE ··············▶

Dear Harlan,
I've given women permission to not want me. I've put myself in rooms, but this doesn't seem to be working. I'm starting to get discouraged. What can I do to keep myself from giving up?
   Still Looking

Dear Still Looking,
Take a break.

Go shopping. Work out. Read a book. Then, go back inside more rooms and take more risks. When you're tired, take a break. Work on your abs. Take a sushi-making class. Hang out with your friends. Then go back inside more rooms and take more risks. When you're tired, take a break and go on a trip. Shave your 'stache, run a half marathon, and take ice-sculpting lessons. Then go back into more rooms. When you're tired, take a break and repeat the process until you find the love of your life. When you want to give up, take a break, change something you don't love, do something interesting, and work to be a better version of you. Then put yourself in more rooms. Eventually, it will happen. When it does, you'll be so interesting and have so many interests that you'll find you miss being single and taking all those breaks.

CHANGE WHAT YOU DON'T LOVE

When you look at yourself in the mirror in your tight thong, you might not like what's hanging out. You have a choice—reject it or accept it. If you want to be successful during your Getting Naked Experiment, rejecting it is no longer an option. In **Step 1** you were introduced to The Universal Rejection Truth of Dating and Relationships. As you take risks and look for love, you'll face a long list of other Truths that you must face and work through.

Take your butt for example. When you put on your tight thong, you may have a hard time acknowledging how your butt looks hanging out of your thong. Should this happen, you'll be faced with a choice. Accept your butt or reject it. While The Universal Rejection Truth of Dating and Relationships says not everyone you want will always want you, The Universal Rejection Truth of Your Butt says that not everyone you want to like your butt will always like your butt. Thousands will find your butt attractive, but millions will not. Some people prefer big butts, small butts, firm butts, soft butts, flat butts, or bubble butts. In the past you might have hidden your butt or attacked anyone who reminded you that your butt was not good enough. This is called living in a state of butt denial. Similar to rejection denial, butt denial is a dark and dangerous place where you think everyone you like should like your butt. If someone doesn't like your butt, there's a big problem. But the problem isn't your butt, it's that you can't give people permission to not like your butt. The even bigger problem is that you don't like your butt. Until you can embrace what's hanging out of your thong, it's unreasonable to expect anyone else to embrace it—that's why it's essential to come out of denial and do some training. Changing what you don't love or changing how you see what you don't love begins with acceptance.

Be prepared to accept:

The Universal Rejection Truth of Your Breasts: not everyone will appreciate your fantastic boobs.

The Universal Rejection Truth of Your Teeth: not everyone will love your beautiful smile.

The Universal Rejection Truth of Your Package: not everyone will want to unwrap your prized package.

The Universal Rejection Truth of Your Sexual Orientation: not everyone will desire your LGBTQ assets.

The Universal Rejection Truth of Your Sexual Experience: not everyone will love your magic move in bed.

The Universal Rejection Truth of Your Drug/Alcohol Use: not everyone will want to date high-flying you.

The Universal Rejection Truth of Your Religion: not everyone will want to be blessed with your presence.

The Universal Rejection Truth of Your Race: not everyone will want to experience your black, white, yellow, red, blue, green, orange, or brown beauty.

The Universal Rejection Truth of Your Profession: not everyone will want to date someone as gainfully employed.

The Universal Rejection Truth of Your Personality: not everyone will want to date someone who has so much or so little of it.

The Universal Rejection Truth of Your Health: not everyone will want to date someone who has overcome as much as you and persevered.

The Universal Rejection Truth of Where You Live: not everyone will want to take a plane, train, bus, or boat to date you.

The Universal Rejection Truth of [fill in the blank]: not everyone will appreciate, include, or desire you for some reason. Their loss. Good thing you live in a world of options.

Similar to accepting The Universal Rejection Truth of Dating and Relationships, in order to change what you don't love or love what you can't change, you must acknowledge what makes you uncomfortable. Once you acknowledge it, you can begin to change or accept it.

Change won't happen in one page of a book. It's a long-term process that may take many attempts and even years to accomplish. As you work to make changes, enlist people in your corner and try new strategies. Once you acknowledge and embrace what's hanging out of your thong:

- Pinpoint what needs to be changed.
- Ask yourself if it's something that can be changed (if it can't be changed, skip ahead to page 93 where Love What You Can't Change begins).
- Ask yourself why you want to change it. Discover if it's holding you back or if how you perceive it is holding you back.
- Turn to people in your corner to help you find answers and an approach to make changes (consider including a doctor, therapist, psychiatrist, nutritionist, trainer, and people who have been there and done it).
- Construct a realistic time line and plan of action (don't set yourself up for disappointment).
- Take action.
- If you can't get the results you desire, change your plan and repeat the process until you get what you want.

Warning #1: Don't make any changes that will compromise your values, character, or closest relationships.

Warning #2: Before getting a butt implant or liposuction, embrace what's hanging out of your emotional thong. Fixing what's hanging out of your emotional thong can turn your physical thong into a much better fit.

Dear Harlan,
I've been cheated on a couple of times in relationships and now I have serious trust issues. Just when something gets good, I have a habit of sabotaging my potential relationship. What can I do to stop this?
   Sabotaging

Dear Sabotaging,
Get obscenely attractive. I mean get ridiculously amazing. Be a better version of yourself. Accumulate so many good qualities (independent of a partner) that no one will ever be able to take them away from you. Then find a great therapist who you can get to know before you start dating. Let that person know your past. Then move forward. Turn to the therapist to make sure you're not making the same mistakes and stay obscenely attractive. Once you have a better relationship with yourself and have someone in your corner whom can you trust, letting someone into your life will be so much easier.

LOVE WHAT YOU CAN'T CHANGE

Some things can't be changed. So you must change how you see them.

If you're a shorter man who wants to be taller you can wear big shoes to give yourself a boost, but you'll still be short in the morning (assuming you don't wear your shoes to bed). On the other hand, some things can be changed, but changing them would mean compromising your values. If you're a virgin saving yourself for marriage, sleeping with someone because you're afraid of losing that person might keep that person around (until he or she gets tired of having sex with you), but it would mean compromising your values. You should be comfortable enough in your I'm Going to Be a Virgin Until Marriage thong to not get into bed with someone out of fear.

When you can't change or won't change what's hanging out of your thong, you have a choice. You can be miserable and blame it for everything that goes wrong in your life, or you can learn to love it. There are three ways to do this:

1. Turn it into an asset. A bigger butt can turn into more to love. Protruding ears can become something to hold on to. Your virginity can turn into the ultimate gift to give. Being bipolar can mean being fun half the time.

2. Get help. It's unrealistic to think that you can flip a switch and embrace the most uncomfortable, traumatic, and difficult parts of your life after reading a few pages in a book.

Someone battling depression can't just get happy. An addict can't (always) just get sober. A rape survivor can't just get over it. That's why there are experts and support systems in place. This book can help you face the truth, but other books and professionals will enable you to manage these issues and not let them get in your way. The things causing you pain or shame, making you lie, cover up, and pretend to be something you're not are the things hanging out of your thong that need to be addressed, explored, and managed.

3. Accept that embracing the things hanging out of your thong will help you attract the right people. The more you train physically, emotionally, and spiritually, the less these things will matter. Do not let one part of you define all of you. The more accepting you can be of what you don't love, the sooner you can find others who will do the same. Focus on your best qualities and trust others will do the same.

We all have a path. Loving what you can't change will help you find the love of your life and live an authentic life you love living.

HOW TO LOVE WHAT YOU CAN'T CHANGE

1. Acknowledge what's hanging out of your thong.
2. Embrace what you can't change.
3. If you can't embrace it, seek professional help.
4. Find people who have been there and done it. Draw inspiration from their tips and their stories.
5. Be kind to yourself. Once you begin to embrace what's in your thong you will be perfectly attractive.

NAKED ADVICE · · · · · · · · · · · · ▷

Dear Harlan,
I was diagnosed with herpes three months ago. I got it from my cheating ex. I can't help but feel like no one will want me. I feel like I'm lying and deceiving people if I don't tell them about my situation before they date me. It's not fair to trick someone. How can I let someone ever get close to me? Will anyone ever want me?
   Scarred from an Ex

Dear Scarred from an Ex,
What a selfish asshole.
   Herpes won't keep you from finding love. Obsessing about it will. Millions of people have herpes and happy

lives. Once you get past the shock and anger you'll find a forgiving world that can love you. You're not doomed. You just have to talk about sex before having it. People who are looking for a meaningless hookup might think twice, but people who are looking for something with meaning will not. So, now, you find out if people want to sleep with you or date you. If you're looking for meaningless sex (no such thing), you can still find it with millions of people who have herpes (one in five adults) or people who don't care if they get it (but those people might give you something else). You're not doomed; you're just forced to talk about sex before you have it. And if you choose, the selfish asshole ex-boyfriend who gave it to you.

SEX FACT #121

Men who have two to four sexual partners in their lifetime have a 3 percent chance of contracting a sexually transmitted infection; women have a 5 percent chance. Men with more than 20 partners have a 28 percent risk of contracting a sexually transmitted infection; women have a 35 percent chance.

Source: *Sex in America,* by Edward Laumann, Robert T. Michael, and Gina Kolata

NAKED ADVICE ·············▶

Dear Harlan,
Whenever I approach women at bars or in random places,
I always imagine them talking about how they couldn't
believe "that guy" approached them. For example, I talked
to this girl and she was so busy looking at her phone during
the entire conversation that I couldn't help but feel like I
bored her. How can I stop thinking everyone is thinking the
worst about me?
    Something to Talk About

Dear Something to Talk About,
If you think you're ugly, creepy, and the worst, you'll
assume these women are thinking the same thing. If you
think you're hot, intriguing, and someone worth knowing,
that's what you'll assume they're thinking when you walk
away. If you thought you were good enough and hot
enough, when the woman looked down at her phone you
could have asked for her number so you could text her
while you talked to her. Then you could have explained
that you do your best work while texting and talking at the
same time. This would either be funny or annoying. It
might have given her something to talk about or a reason
to run. If she didn't run, she might have shared that she
was waiting for a text from her doctor to get test results
(awkward). Or she might have given you her number. Until

you are at your very best, you'll always think the very worst.

YOU DON'T NEED TO CREEP, PLOT, PLAN, DRINK, OR PUKE

Your Getting Naked Experiment will prove to be liberating.

Once you embrace The Universal Rejection Truth of Dating and Relationships, train in your thongs, and have options, you won't need to get caught up in the minutiae and drama (aka games). You won't need to keep track of who texted whom, how long he or she waited between texts, and how long you need to wait. You won't have to read into text subtext and get emotional about emoticons. When you know there are options and aren't afraid to express yourself, these things matter less. There isn't time or energy for it to matter.

Talking to people you want to meet will no longer take a few shots or a few beers. You don't have to get wasted to find the courage to speak. You don't have to sleep with someone to get to know someone. It won't take weeks, months, or years of hanging out in the same room with the same people to say what you feel. You don't have to creep on someone's Facebook and look through someone's pictures to determine if that person is hugging a cousin, sibling, or significant other. If you're interested in someone, you'll express yourself sooner and while sober. You won't keep feelings a secret because you're scared of getting rejected or worried about making someone uncomfortable. You will no longer need to creep, plot, plan, or silently obsess—because you will be too busy exploring other opportunities with other people to invest so much time and energy.

Once you take the risk and find the love of your life, you'll find it safer and easier to express yourself inside the relationship. When someone or something bothers you, instead of hating, hiding, ignoring, resenting, excusing, cheating, or doing something you'll later regret, you can deal with it. When you live in a world of options and have the emotional stamina to handle whatever comes your way, keeping your feelings a secret is far riskier than sharing the truth.

NAKED ADVICE ·············▶

Dear Harlan,
I met the perfect guy at a friend's party a few weeks ago. We talked, texted, and became Facebook friends the next day. He says we should go out, but he hasn't asked me. He appears to be close with another girl, or that's what I've surmised based on her Facebook posts. She writes on his wall. He's also in pictures with her. His relationship status is complicated, but he says he's single. Sometimes I'll text him and he doesn't text back until the next day, but he'll post status updates on his wall. It makes me think he's not interested. But then he'll stop by my work and flirt with me and make it seem like he's interested. It's all starting to drive me crazy. I can't stop thinking about him. Any advice?
    Runaround

Dear Runaround,
It might help to create an Excel spreadsheet to track your
texts and his Facebook posts. Be sure to cross-reference
with Twitter (you might have missed his tweets). Then print
out his Facebook pictures and craft a family tree and a
friendship tree to identify all possible relationships. While
you're working on the trees, set up Google alerts to see if
there are any discussions where his name or e-mail is
mentioned. When you're finished with these projects, if
you're still unclear, consider seeing a psychic. If that doesn't
help, consider looking to date one of the thousands of other
men who will text you back, call you, and take you out.
This guy might be taking up too much of your time.

YOU'LL WANT A COMPLEMENT, NOT JUST COMPLIMENTS

Once you embrace The Truth and train in your thong you no longer need compliments to validate you, but rather, you'll want
someone to complement you. A compliment is different than a
complement. A compliment would be, "Hey, nice ass." (Not the
classiest compliment.) A complement completes you and makes
you feel whole. Once you go through this process, you already
know you're good enough. You don't need someone to prop you
up to feel good enough. A relationship is no longer a crutch to
keep you from limping through life. Once you know you're good
enough, you don't need to win people over or do things you will

later regret to keep someone interested (i.e., drunk sex in a bathroom at a bar). You can spend less time thinking about who wants YOU and more time focusing on what YOU want. It's a totally different way of looking at dating and relationships.

COMPLIMENT VS. COMPLEMENT

Compliment: an expression of esteem, respect, affection, or admiration

Complement: something that fills up, completes, or makes perfect

Once you're in a relationship, you will be able to stand on your own two feet. You don't have to worry about losing your crutch. When something makes you uncomfortable, you don't need to ignore it because you're afraid of feeling defective or losing your significant other. Likewise, when something makes your partner uncomfortable, you will want to know and listen without hating, getting defensive, or hiding from The Truth. Being able to stand on your own two feet means that you can face The Truth—no matter how painful it might be. One more perk that comes with embracing The Truth and training in your thongs—you won't get as jealous. You won't worry your boyfriend or girlfriend will find someone better because you know they already have the best.

Finally, should a relationship end, you will never fall as hard. Yes, you'll still hurt, but when you know you're good enough and have a life outside of the relationship, you can recover faster, even after getting punched in the gut. Should you ever forget you're good enough, the people in your corner can pick you up and help you move forward.

NAKED ADVICE · · · · · · · · · · · ·➤

Dear Harlan,
I've been in a great relationship for three months, but can't seem to relax. I'm waiting for the bottom to fall out and for the person I'm dating to realize this isn't going to work. I find myself wanting to sabotage things so I can be the one to end it. I want to relax. I have no reason to doubt the relationship, but that's not working. What can I do to get over this habit of ruining good things?
    Anxious

Dear Anxious,
It's like getting out of a perfectly safe car and walking home alone because you're afraid of car accidents. If you wear a seat belt, avoid texting behind the wheel, and drive at safe speeds you still might get rear-ended once in a while, but not wrecked. The problem is that for most people, dating ends in a wreck because they don't know how to do it safely. Here's how you create a safe way to experience the wild dating ride: Have a life independent of this relationship. Have interests that belong to you. Have friends that never go away (I don't mean to take them on dates with you).

Make sure you are comfortable in your skin and know you are good enough to date. With safeguards in place, you can take the top down and have the ride of your life.

HOOKING UP WILL NEVER FEEL THE SAME AGAIN

When you're comfortable in your thongs, you can be much more discerning about who you let see you in your thong.

The reason hooking up is so common is because most people don't have the balls or ovaries to be honest with the people who interest them. A hookup is just a back door into relationships. You can make a connection without having to share your feelings or open yourself up to getting hurt before connecting.

Once you embrace The Universal Rejection Truth and get comfortable in your thongs, hooking up will not give you the same thrill it did before. You will know you're good enough, and when you know you're good enough, having sex with a random person isn't a big turn-on. It can be a turnoff. Having a relationship becomes easier and much more satisfying.

Should your Getting Naked Experiment lead to getting naked, it will also be different. You will find it easier to talk about sex before, during, and after having it. You won't hesitate to talk about someone's history and what to expect after having the sex. During the sex, you will say what feels right. You will say what feels wrong. You will also avoid post-sex drama and confusion. Should a hookup end too soon or a relationship end with a breakup, having options and feeling good enough in your thong means not feeling regret, not running back to exes, and never making excuses for inexcusable behavior.

And that's how dating becomes easier than hooking up.

NAKED ADVICE ·············➤

Dear Harlan,
My way-too-hot female good friend wants to be friends with benefits. This wouldn't normally be a problem, but I have stronger feelings for her. I'd like to be in a relation- ship. I told her I could be friends with benefits, but only if she would be open to something more. Do you think this is a good idea?
  Purely Sexual

Dear Purely Sexual,
Being friends with benefits feels good during the sex. Once the sex ends, the good idea ends, too.

If you're looking for more than sex, don't have it and expect more than she can give. There's just no way you can have sex with her one day and then hear about her new crush on the next. The greatest part of this situation is that you two seem to be able to talk honestly before getting naked. Until you both get what you want out of this, there is no benefit to having sex. Unless you're looking to have sex with a hot friend for a while and never talk to her again.

YOU CAN FIND THOUSANDS OF PEOPLE
WHO WANT TO DATE YOU

Before training, hooking up and dating were mostly a series of fortunate accidents. You didn't know where, when, or how the hell it happened. When it did happen, there was a tendency to go too fast or hang on to it way too tight for way too long. That's part of not having control over the process. Once you've trained and are comfortable with The Truth, this all changes.

You can clearly see how and where it happens. It most frequently happens in rooms where people spend a lot of time sharing common experiences—offices, classrooms, and neighborhoods. It also happens in places single people hang out—online dating sites, singles' events, and parties with single people. It can happen in rooms when people share feelings with people they don't know very well—retail love, commuter encounters, and coffee shop connections. It also happens when people speak up and ask for friends to help—fix-ups, double dates, parties, etc. And it happens in rooms with alcohol—bars, parties, weddings, and other events. If you want it to happen while sober, put yourself in rooms, talk to people in rooms, ask people to help you meet people in rooms, and do things you love to do with people who love doing the same things in a lot of different rooms for a long period of time. When you fully embrace The Universal Rejection Truths of life, train in your thongs, and surround yourself with people who want you to win, you will find what you want.

It's hard to predict precisely when it will happen, but it will. And it will happen again and again. Now, if you want it to happen, you can make it happen. Dating and relationships happen not because people are lucky, but because people put themselves in the path of opportunity. Now that you've trained and are comfortable with the process, it will be easier to make it happen when you want it to happen because you have the emotional stamina to put yourself in the path of opportunity over and over again. With patience, persistence, and faith it will happen.

Now you never need to be scared of being single or stay in unhealthy relationships. You can demand and command respect before, during, and after a relationship. If someone doesn't treat you the way you deserve to be treated, you will speak up sooner rather than later. If someone breaks up with you, you will feel sad and then you'll find someone else. The world is filled with options. Never again do you have to settle or make excuses. That phase of your life is officially in the past.

NAKED ADVICE • • • • • • • • • • • • • ▶

Dear Harlan,
I finally told my longtime friend I have feelings for him.
He told me he loves hanging out with me but I'm not his
type. He generally doesn't date women who are bigger than
him. He tried to make light of it, but I'm devastated and
disappointed in him! I've liked him for a long time. I'm
shocked to find out that he's just another asshole guy.
   Too Big

Dear Too Big,
At least he's an honest asshole. You have three choices: get
smaller, get him to like bigger, or get over it. Millions of men
love bigger women. He's not one of them. Don't blame him.
He told you the truth. Give him permission to be attracted
to women with a different physique. Appreciate that he
feels connected enough to be honest with you. I mean, he
could have slept with you to try it out, and then told you
the truth. Now, that's an asshole move. Once you get over
the hurt, keep him around. Honest friends are hard to find.
And you never know, he might discover smaller women
can't compete with all the bigger things you have to offer.

ASSHOLES, BITCHES, AND COUPLES IN LOVE WILL NO LONGER SUCK

Soon, you'll be too busy to hate people or call them names.

Of course, you will still run into the occasional asshole or bitch (I hate this word) during your Getting Naked Experiment, but it will be different now. You might not even call them names. Giving people permission to not want you means not having to hate people or hide from them. Having options means not wasting time on the wrong people. Feeling good enough about yourself means not taking it so personally. And being able to freely share your feelings means you will move on and find other places to put your energy.

Once you do find someone worth your time, if that person

turns into an asshole or bitch, you'll say something the first time it happens. The second time, you'll do something and end it. Now that you have options and know how to go after what you want, you don't need to put up with this crap. You'll be far less tolerant and way too busy exploring other opportunities.

When you do get hurt by an asshole or bitch, it will still hurt, but not as bad for as long. It's more like a stubbed toe than a broken bone. No one should ever hurt you, but once you're trained, you'll recognize that the people who hurt you are just terribly uncomfortable in their thongs. Their actions say more about them than you. And that's when anger gives way to compassion and forgiveness. Understanding this will mean you won't scar as badly, you won't have to put up walls to protect yourself, and you won't settle for exes just because you're too afraid you'll get hurt again by someone else.

As for couples in love—some will be inspiring, and some just sad. Having a relationship doesn't mean being happy in it. It just means someone was in a room long enough and found someone.

NAKED ADVICE · · · · · · · · · · · · ▶

Dear Harlan,
I'm a virgin and my boyfriend wants to have sex. We've been together for a few months. I really love him. I was planning on waiting until I got married, but he says he loves me, too, and needs a sexual relationship. Any advice?
   Still Waiting

Dear Still Waiting,
If he needs to have sex so badly he can find someone else to
pressure into having sex or have sex alone. Want to see if
he really loves you? Wait. If you do start having sex and he
tells you doing it with a condom isn't real sex, get a real
boyfriend. Or you can have real sex and a real problem when
you get really pregnant and he splits. No one worth dating
will pressure or ask you to do something that feels wrong.

ONCE YOU'VE TRAINED . . . YOU WILL DATE, BUT NEVER SETTLE

Now that you've accepted The Truth, trained in your thongs, and have options, you can find your best choice—not your only choice. You can get to know yourself and others on a new level. You'll date so you can figure out what you like and don't like. You'll date to have experiences. You'll get to know people and allow them to know you. You'll have more fun with more people. The more vulnerable you allow yourself to be during your Getting Naked Experiment, the better the results. The more comfortable you can get in your thongs, the easier it will be to find strong connections and find someone you can grow with while encouraging each other to be your personal best.

Once trained, relationships will unfold naturally. Getting married won't be about running away from being single, but a decision based on wanting to build a life with someone you like, and love. Liking someone will be as important as loving them. When you like being with someone (while clothed and sober), you can stay in love. The naked and drunk part is easy. Now, you have time and room to get to know someone and let someone get to know you. Enjoy every minute of it.

Getting Naked will help you and your partner really get to know each other in your respective thongs before moving forward. Think about the life span of a relationship; two people meet, date, fall in love, get engaged, and get married before really knowing each other in all of their thongs. It can be six months of dating, nine months of planning a wedding, and a year in the honeymoon phase—that's about two years of heightened emotions and celebrations. If you have a kid, add another year of focusing on something other than the relationship. I'm not saying you can't meet someone and get married in a short amount of time—it can happen and work out well. But it will work out best when two people are comfortable in their thongs before meeting, know what they like, and are at their personal bests. That's when you know you're with your best choice, not your only choice. And that's when you know you'll never settle for anything but the best.

NAKED ADVICE   ·············▶

Dear Harlan,
I'm nineteen years old and just got engaged. I've been dating my boyfriend for three years and we have the best relationship. My friends and family think I should wait, but I don't see a reason for waiting when we know we've found the best possible partners for ourselves. Any advice?
   Blissfully Engaged

Dear Blissfully Engaged,
No cops at the wedding—it will spoil your champagne toast
if you and the groom are under twenty-one. This might be
the best relationship or the worst, but unless there is a
religious reason to get married or you're pregnant, I'd enjoy
a long engagement. Why not date a few more years? Take
time to know who you are and what you want. It's hard to
be a couple when you've barely had time to be an individual.
Sometimes, getting married young is more about running
from being single than running into a relationship that will
last forever. At the very least, make it a long engagement
and wait until you can legally toast your bliss.

YOU'RE ALMOST READY FOR YOUR GETTING NAKED EXPERIMENT TO BEGIN

Once you accept and embrace The Universal Rejection Truth of Dating and Relationships, train in your thong(s), know you have options, and get the right people in your corner, you'll almost be ready to start your Getting Naked Experiment. The five things you learned during your informal relationship education, the things that set you up for drama and disaster, will no longer hold you back, confuse you, or keep you in bad relationships.

Here's what's changed since the start of the book:

BEFORE: Sharing your feelings used to be too dangerous.
NOW: Keeping your feelings secret is too dangerous.

BEFORE: You didn't feel good enough.

NOW: No one can make you feel defective. You know you are attractive, desirable, and good enough.

BEFORE: Hooking up was faster and easier than dating.

NOW: Dating is just as fast as hooking up and far less of a headache. Always.

BEFORE: You didn't know where, when, or how IT all happened.

NOW: Now you know how IT happens. You know where IT happens (in rooms). You just don't know when IT will happen.

BEFORE: Men were assholes, women were bitches, and couples in love sucked.

NOW: You have too many options and too little time to waste on calling people names.

Stop Making Excuses

I know ... I know ...

You don't know if he's single, you don't know if she's interested, you don't want to lose the friendship, you don't want to get fired, you don't want to look creepy, you don't like long-distance relationships, you don't do online dating, you don't do setups, you don't want to get hurt, you don't have time for games, you don't have time, period, you aren't looking for someone right now, and you are happy being single (then, why are you reading this book?).

Step 3: It's time to stop bullshitting yourself.

Now that you've embraced The Universal Rejection Truth and trained in your thongs, you can see that excuses are nothing more than baggy sweatpants—they're all about covering up the insecurities hanging out of our thongs. Excuses are self-imposed roadblocks to keep us from feeling vulnerable and getting hurt. Instead of letting them hold you back, let them lead you to answers. When you feel an excuse coming, look in the mirror, put on your thong, and figure out what's hanging out. If you can't find answers or an approach that works, get help from people in your corner.

DO NOT LET EXCUSES STOP YOU. Think of me as someone in your corner reminding you of all the things you need to

hear, but might not always want to hear. I want you to be successful. I want you to win. If you have a question about this step or
this book, send me a note. If it's an excuse, don't bother. I want to
help you find answers—not take up more time while you make
more excuses. Send your notes to harlan@helpmeharlan.com or
via www.gettingnakedexperiment.com.

NAKED ADVICE ·············▶

Dear Harlan,
I went on a date with a girl I liked a lot the other night. My
problem is that she slept with me. I was disappointed
because I have a rule that I will not date a girl who sleeps
with me on the first date. It means she probably sleeps with
other guys on the first date. And that's not the type of
woman I want to date. Why is it that women think sleeping
with a guy on a first date will get them a second date?
   A Man with Standards

Dear Man with Standards,
Maybe SHE was using you because SHE knows you're a big
slut. Or maybe she was the one testing you to see if you'd
sleep with her on the first date because she actually wanted
to date you. And you failed. Then again, she might have
actually felt a strong connection with you and wanted to
share something special with you—something she NEVER

does on a first date. Instead of making excuses why not to date her, ask her if she's done this before. Then be prepared to have her ask you the same. You might want to date her. You might even want to marry her. That is, if she can respect you enough to date you.

EXCUSE #1: I'M TOO SHY TO APPROACH SOMEONE

You're only shy until you know someone likes you, right?

That's not *really* called shy—it's called being stuck in rejection denial and being uncomfortable in your thong. As you conduct your Getting Naked Experiment, you might find yourself reluctant to approach people. You might say, "I'm just shy." In the past, shy would be good enough to stop you—but no more. Here's why shy has changed since you've started this book: Once you accept The Universal Rejection Truth, you give people permission to think freely and no longer worry what they are thinking. When you train in your thong(s), you are your personal best and know you're good enough, regardless of what other people think. Therefore, you no longer need to be afraid of people not liking you. Once you're no longer afraid, you can't call yourself shy.

Follow that thinking?

You can have a hard time meeting people, dislike online dating, not want to come off as creepy, not want to lose a friendship, be afraid of approaching people you don't know, be concerned you'll get hurt, be worried you'll lose your job, be unsure if someone is single, be old-fashioned, hate dating, lack experience, not like being set up, dis-like long-distance relationships, not want to hurt people's feelings, be very picky, and not want to settle, but don't call yourself shy.

It's not true.

◆ **Naked Suggestion:** If you finish this book and are still too un-comfortable to say what you feel, get a psychologist, therapist, or counselor in your corner to help. You might have a social anxiety disorder or other issue that needs professional attention.

NAKED ADVICE ··············▶

Dear Harlan,
What's the best way to approach a girl who's extremely shy? I don't want to scare this person off. I think we could be a perfect couple.
  Shy Approach

Dear Shy,
What makes her perfect? Ahhh, I know all too well.
  I used to be very attracted to shy women, too. I loved the fact they didn't have the confidence to approach other guys. I found that sexy. I figured, if a shy girl liked me, she would be too shy to find anyone else. It was safe. I could rescue her. I could be her sole source of self-confidence. Now, I find it scary. I prefer confident women. I've seen shy women grow up and realize they have options—and a

girl who has options can break a guy's heart if he's not her best choice. To answer the question, approach a shy person just like you'd approach anyone. If you scare her, wait until she's not so shy and approach her again. The last thing you want is to start a relationship having to tiptoe around someone's emotions.

BIGGEST DATING FEAR #902

I'm mostly afraid of getting rejected. I try anyway, and I end up getting rejected, which doesn't help my fear. I'm a really shy person, so it's difficult to open myself up like that, and it gets harder each time when someone doesn't want me.

EXCUSE #2: I NEVER KNOW WHAT TO SAY

I know the perfect pickup line. But I can't give it to you. I could, but it might not be the perfect line for you. Then you'd use the excuse that I gave you the wrong line and you'd blame me for you being single and searching.

If you want to know what to say, define your role before speaking. For example, when you order a drink at a coffee shop, you know your role. You are the customer. You tell the person behind the counter what you want. The person behind the counter listens and gives you what you want. You both have your roles. During the transaction, you can ask a question (Really, $5.25 for a mocha latte?), share an observation (Damn, that's an expensive mocha latte.), or talk about something interesting (Let me treat you to a mocha latte. It's less than a beer.). You can be friendly, funny, smart, boring, or offensive. After a few laughs and thousands of dollars of mocha lattes, you might find yourself getting served a lot of mocha latte in bed.

While finding love isn't the same as placing an order (unless you're in Vegas at a legal brothel), once you define your role, you'll know what to say. Your role during your Getting Naked Experiment is as follows: You are attractive, single and searching, and looking for a meaningful relationship. What you say will be directly related to what you feel and what you think (brilliant, right?). Ask a question, offer a compliment, or make an observation. Just say hello and smile. Remind yourself before approaching someone that anyone who meets you is lucky to be in your life. This isn't cocky or arrogant; it's confident and self-assured. Confident people care what other people think. Cocky and arrogant people don't. If you're ever uncomfortable in your role, take a step back, look at yourself in your thong, and make changes. The more comfortable you become in your single and searching role, the easier it will be to have conversations with people while taking everyday risks.

◆ **Need More Help Figuring Out What To Say? Step 4** will break down fifteen risks and help you define your role so you can find the words.

NAKED ADVICE · · · · · · · · · · · ·➤

Dear Harlan,
I'm looking for the perfect pickup line. I haven't had a lot of luck in the dating department. Any help would be appreciated.
Single and Searching

Dear Single and Searching,

YOU: (approaching woman) *Excuse me, do you like magic?*

WOMAN: *Yes, I love magic!*

YOU: *Great, touch me right here.* (point to your arm)

WOMAN: *Okay.*

YOU: *Now, kiss me right here.* (point to your cheek)

WOMAN: *Okay.* (she burps)

YOU: *Now, say the magic words, "Pantsoff! Pantsoff! Pantsoff!" and watch my pants disappear.*

WOMAN: *Pants off! Pants off! Pants . . .* (she passes out drunk)

NOTE: *This works best on desperate women, drunk women, and drunk and desperate women who are hard of hearing.*

Another approach is to say what you're thinking. Don't try to pick up women—try to get to know them. A compliment, an observation, or a simple "hello" done with the right sentiment and smile is all it takes.

BEST PICKUP LINE #702

"Do you have the time?" (I gave him the time) "No, the time to write my number down." It was cute and it broke the ice without being creepy or perverted like most lines.

EXCUSE #3: I'M OLD-FASHIONED (AKA I DON'T DO THE APPROACHING)

Your grandma didn't sit on Facebook waiting for someone to poke her.

Some of you will hide behind the excuse that you're old-fashioned. In other words, you expect everyone else to do the approaching. I have one word for you—old. You risk getting old waiting for someone to approach you. Some women think a man should be the one to make the first move. They think men who don't make the first move do not deserve their attention. But let me tell you, some of the most loving men don't want to approach you because they don't want to make you uncomfortable. And really, a lot of you don't make yourself all that approachable.

Still, there will be women who read this who won't budge. Fine. But you're missing out. Let the same people approach you in the same old places. Then have the same old conversations with the same old friends about how you want to know where all the good guys are hiding. Here's a secret. Come closer. Closer . . . THEY

ARE ALL AROUND YOU. Talk to them. Make it clear you're interested.

You can still be old-fashioned and be assertive. Starting a conversation and making it clear you're interested is one way old-fashioned women can meet old-fashioned men. Post an online profile that says you're old-fashioned. Make it clear that you want someone to do the approaching. At least make it clear that you're safe to approach and what you want. If you want something old-fashioned, ask a friend to set you up. Women can approach men, men can approach women, women can approach women, men can approach men, and all can have their dignity and respect after starting a conversation.

What so many old-fashioned women don't understand is that many old-fashioned men are bad at approaching women. They don't want to get hurt or upset you. Now that parents no longer arrange marriages or make appointments for men to call on women things must change. Some men are old-fashioned gentlemen callers who need old-fashioned women to let them know it's okay to court them. If you make yourself available and give people access to you, you will be approached. If you don't want to look desperate, explain that you're not a woman who typically does the approaching while doing the approaching. If you're a man who doesn't want to be too assertive, consider that lady you have your eye on might be old-fashioned and need an assertive man. Old-fashioned doesn't have to mean growing old alone. You can be forward and still be old-fashioned—call it old-fashioned-forward.

NAKED ADVICE · · · · · · · · · · · ·▶

Dear Harlan,
I've tried to approach men, but I'm afraid of looking
desperate or getting used. How can I still maintain my
dignity and approach a man without appearing too
thirsty? I'm not thirsty, just tired of waiting around.
   Old-Fashioned

Dear Old-Fashioned,
No oral sex in bathroom stalls with men you just meet—it
makes you look desperate and will leave you feeling used.
   Men need more women like you. Understand that
some of the best men are too polite to make a first move.
Help them safely approach you by making it clear what
you want. When you see a man who interests you, help
him know you're open to being approached. Start a
conversation. Then, say it in the clearest terms: "We
should hang out." Give him your e-mail, number, or
Twitter handle. Men need women to be obvious. Clear a
direct path to you. Then, if you're thirsty, let him buy you
a drink.

BEST DATE EVER #512

I suggested a walk around the park, which ended up being right after a huge rainstorm. There were huge puddles all over and I talked my date into taking off his socks and shoes to jump in puddles with me. Then he took me out for ice cream and we chatted for several hours.

EXCUSE #4: IT'S HARD TO MEET PEOPLE

It used to be hard.

Once you embrace The Universal Rejection Truth and train in your thongs, instead of seeing opportunities to get hurt and avoid taking risks, you'll see opportunities to have good experiences and take more risks. This will help you meet more people and make your world much bigger.

Once you *want* to meet more people and make the effort, you will. You'll meet them when you approach them. You'll meet them when you spend time in more rooms with them. You'll meet them while dating online, getting set up, and doing things you love to do with other people. It will be easier to meet people because you'll make the time and effort to meet them. It will be a priority.

If you have a hard time meeting the *right* people, you'll try harder and be more resourceful. You'll find other ways to meet them. You'll put yourself in different rooms with different people.

You'll turn to friends, family, classmates, and coworkers to set you up. You'll join groups, organizations, and get involved in activities with people who share your values and approach to life. If you live in a smaller community, you'll expand your search area and meet more people in other cities, states, and countries. If you have a medical issue that makes it harder to meet people, you'll find a support group or an approach that will make it easier for the right people to get to know you. If you don't have the time, you'll find and make the time. If you find there just aren't enough people to meet, you'll change your criteria and explore more options. You won't stop until you find what you want.

When you feel good about yourself and are open to meeting people, it's hard to avoid them. They come to you. The moment you feel good enough and want to meet people, you can and will meet people.

NAKED ADVICE · · · · · · · · · · · ·➤

> *Dear Harlan,*
> *I'm having a hard time meeting people. Almost all of the people I work with are married or too old for me. The closest big city is sixty miles away. I work sixty hours a week. I don't want to do online dating because I'm a private person. How can I meet someone given that I barely have time for myself and don't want to settle? I want to find a partner before my eggs shrivel up!*
> *Missing the Meeting*

Dear Missing the Meeting,
Change your approach and don't mention your shriveling eggs on the first date (even if it's a breakfast date).

Here's how you change the approach: get fixed up, date online, date long distance, use a high-end dating service, travel to singles' spots during your vacation, work with younger people, get involved in organizations for young professionals, date older people, attend a lot of weddings with single people, move to a more populated city, change careers, change the hours you work, work to be your hottest, drive to meet people, fly to meet people, take boats to meet people, make time to meet people, get set up, go online, have faith, and change your attitude. Until you commit to making some changes and go after what you want, it will be hard to meet people. If you are working sixty hours a week, you are a passionate person. Put some of that passion into finding someone who will appreciate you and your eggs.

GETTING NAKED TIP #169

If you don't dance, don't try meeting someone at a dance club. If you hate sports, don't try meeting someone while playing something athletic. If you've never met people at bars, don't start trying; meet people doing things you love to do and feel comfortable doing. Be kind to yourself and use your strengths to meet people. Set yourself up for success.

EXCUSE #5: I DON'T WANT TO LOOK CREEPY

I know you're not creepy (wait . . . are you?).

Even if you're the kindest, caring, and most well-intentioned person, you have the potential to appear creepy when approaching someone. Accept it. As long as you're not doing your approaching in the middle of the night, in a dark alley, while wearing a trench coat, appreciate that the only way to avoid the creepy factor is to avoid talking to people—and that's not an option if you want to be successful.

Give people permission to think you're creepy. Remind yourself that part of playing the role of a single and searching person is possibly looking creepy. As long as you're not scary creepy there isn't anything more to discuss. If you're not sure what it means to be scary creepy, I'll help you out. Scary creepy would be:

◆ Approaching people while wasted at night in dark alleys
◆ Approaching people while sober at night in dark alleys
◆ Talking about sex during a first conversation
◆ Sexting pictures of your penis, vagina, or bulging parts
◆ Sharing too much information too soon (no one needs to know your complete medical history on a first date)
◆ Talking about an ex incessantly (actually, that's just annoying)
◆ Following people to places without their knowledge
◆ Following people to places with their knowledge
◆ Dating people without their knowledge (think Facebook)

◆ Showing up uninvited in someone's personal space (home, gym, work, etc.)

◆ Threatening to hurt someone who doesn't like you

As long as you have good intentions, accept that your best of intentions might be misunderstood at times. Someone may need time to get to know you. The love of your life could think you're a creep at first—accept it.

◆ **Warning:** If your good intentions are misunderstood all the time, turn to the people in your corner. You might discover you are accidentally scary creepy.

NAKED ADVICE ·············▶

Dear Harlan,
I get what you're saying about The Universal Rejection Truth, but approaching a random stranger and saying, "Do you want to see a movie?" sounds creepy to me. I'm not sure how to do the approaching.
  Not Creepy

Dear Not Creepy,
That might be creepy, especially if you're not wearing pants. Even with pants, a person might find it creepy to be asked to a movie by a total stranger. I'd start with a conversation. You could say, "If I knew you better, I'd ask you to a

movie. I bet you'd like to see . . ." Acknowledge that you don't know someone, but then give someone a chance to know you. Ask for directions (even if you know where to go). Ask for a restaurant suggestion (even if you know where to eat). Ask the time (even if your cell has the time). Say something. Start a conversation. If you're uncomfortable while doing the approaching, mention that you don't want to interrupt or make that person uncomfortable, but if you didn't say something now, you might miss the chance forever. Confidence, sobriety, and daylight reduce the creepy factor—and yes, wearing pants helps, too.

CREEPIEST DATING MOMENT #416

He said to me, "You remind me of my mom." Ugh. No woman needs to hear that, especially when she's getting undressed. That killed the mood.

EXCUSE #6: I CAN'T TELL IF SOMEONE IS SINGLE

Does it matter?

There might be a time during your Getting Naked Experiment when you will want to approach someone and not know if that person is single. Unfortunately, relationship statuses aren't posted on people's foreheads (just on their social networking profiles).

The best way to find out if someone is single is to approach that person and start a conversation. If you meet someone who tells you, "I'm in a relationship," be cool. Respond with, "Not a surprise. I can't imagine someone like you being single for long." Then, consider a friendship. That's what it means to be comfortable in your thong and accepting of The URT.

Here's what you need to know—a lot of people in relationships don't stay in relationships forever. Some get married, but most do not. The best time to start a friendly relationship can be when someone is in a relationship. This can be the perfect time to see how that person behaves in a relationship. You can learn about their strengths and insecurities. You can see if someone is faithful and honest. You can also observe if it's a strong relationship or barely surviving. You won't get laid, but that's not the goal.

If someone in a relationship offers you friendship don't run from the friend zone. Give it enough time and your friend will be single again. And then you can make your feelings known again; that is, if you're still interested. Don't worry about getting stuck in the friend zone. Now that you have gone through the first two steps in this book, you'll never allow someone to stick you anywhere you don't belong.

NAKED ADVICE · · · · · · · · · · · ·➤

Dear Harlan,
I met a girl on the bus while commuting to work. She wears a lot of jewelry. She appears to be kind of artsy. She has a ring on her ring finger and I can't tell if she's engaged,

married, or just into her own look. We've been playing
the I-look-at-you-and-then-you-look-at-me game. I'm
interested in talking to her, but don't know if she's single.
Would a single girl wear a ring on her wedding finger? Is
there some rule about this?
   Ringer

Dear Ringer,
*She does it to confuse you and all us men. (Note to women:
we don't know the difference between a ring on your left
hand or right hand. No rings on ring fingers. Rings on toes
will not confuse us. Even your ring finger toe.)*

   *As for the advice, ask her about it. If she's married, ask
if she has a sister. If she's single, tell her that you like her
taste in jewelry. Let her know that if you get along, you'll
be sure to get her a ring that goes with the rest of her
jewelry. Just tell her what you're thinking and go from
there. Either way, you'll find out something you didn't
know before. And who knows, she might have a single sister
with an available ring finger for you.*

REGRETTABLE SEXUAL MOMENT #96

We were in the middle of having sex when he told me he
had a confession—he was married! Needless to say, the sex
ended on the spot.

REGRETTABLE SEXUAL MOMENT #97

He said to me, "These were my ex's favorite type of condoms, I hope that means that you'll like them, too."

EXCUSE #7: I DON'T WANT TO LOSE A FRIENDSHIP

You are so selfish.

Yes, YOU (pointing my finger at you).

You call yourself a friend?

How dare you deprive a good friend of the best thing that could happen to him or her? What kind of friend are you if you're *this* attractive and you do not give your friend a chance to have a piece of you?

That's not a good friend. It's a terrible friend.

If you can't see that you are the opportunity of a lifetime, then you need to turn back to **Step 2** and train in your thong. There might be a valid reason not to share your feelings with your friend, but most of them are temporary. If you're worried about losing the friendship—the most common fear—there are three things you MUST do to make a move and minimize losing a friend:

1. You MUST have more than one friend. If not, you will be in no place to date a friend. If the friend isn't interested

you will risk being friendless, so make sure you have a few more friends before making your move. Training in your thongs and finding people in your corner should give you more friends.

2. You MUST give your friend permission to not want you and just be a friend. You can't just say it or think it—YOU MUST BELIEVE IT. Otherwise, things will get weird if a friend isn't interested. You will be the one to get weird. And then, the friendship will NEVER survive.

3. You MUST know that you have options. If you think there is only one person in the world who can love you and it's your friend, and that friend doesn't give you what you want, you will never get over it. You will hate or hide from your friend, ruining the friendship.

A few other things to consider: If you're looking for random sex, avoid doing it with a friend. All sex has meaning. Unless you're looking to get married, find a fortunate accident. Dating a friend should only happen when you see staying together forever. For suggestions on how to make the move, see Do It with a Friend in **Step 4.**

◆ **A Note to People Who Have Friends Who Express Interest:** Don't make a friend feel like crap because he or she is interested in you. It doesn't have to get weird. Give your friend permission to want you. You don't need to want your friend. You just need to be nice.

NAKED ADVICE · · · · · · · · · · · ·▶

Dear Harlan,
My guy friend of several years just told me he had feelings
for me. I just got out of a bad relationship. I need a friend
right now, not a boyfriend. I don't know how I can be
friends with him now that I know he's interested in more.
It changes how I look at him and hug him. He's like a
brother to me. How can I still be friends when I know he
wants more?
　　　F'ed-Up Friendship

Dear F'ed-Up Friendship,
I feel for this friendly man of yours.
　　This guy can't win. He was doing you a favor. He saw you
in a crappy-ass relationship and thought he could do better
than the other guy. He waited until you were single before
some other asshole swept in. I'm sure his feelings have been
there for a long time. He was polite enough not to share them
while you were dating. Clearly he knows how to be a good
friend and have feelings for you without them being recipro-
cated. He might have surprised you, but don't fault him for it.
Assuming he's given you permission to not want him, this
will only get weird if you allow it to get weird. If he gets weird,
tell him. But he can still be your friend without being your
boyfriend. He's done it for years. Who knows, maybe one day
you'll realize he's a best friend and the best man for you.

EXCUSE #8: I DON'T DO ONLINE DATING

How could you rob the world of a chance to meet someone as hot as you?

If you were single and searching in the 1950s and someone told you that in fifty years there would be a way to browse thousands of profiles of single men and women looking for love, view their pictures, read about their interests, talk to them by sending electronic messages, and speak to them live through your television at home, in your underwear, you'd think that person was crazy. You could only dream meeting people would be so simple.

And here we are in the future, with free and pay services available catering to nearly every niche, need, and desire. We can literally view thousands of pictures, send messages, and talk to people in our underwear. Yet, still, so many single people aren't making themselves available.

Maybe you've done it and didn't like it. Maybe you stopped after one or two bad dates. Maybe you haven't tried it because it's just "not you" (whatever that means). Maybe you've just heard other people's horror stories and avoided it. According to research commissioned by Match.com, approximately one in five relationships start online. If you're attractive, single, and searching, put yourself online. If you've been online, do it again.

Appreciate online dating for what it is—a weird and wild world where being ignored is the norm, goal weights replace real weights, and adding three extra inches to select body parts is accepted. As you participate in your Getting Naked Experiment, date online.

Don't stop after a few weeks or a few bad dates. Allow people to find you. Explore different services every few months. Change your profile regularly to attract and find different types of people. Be patient and date to have fun. The goal is to have interesting experiences. Just like any kind of dating, sometimes it won't work. But a lot of times, it will.

If you're worried about rejection—that's no longer a valid excuse. In the past, online dating was the equivalent of turning yourself into a human punching bag. But now, you have embraced The Universal Rejection Truth and trained in your thong, so you are equipped to take part in an imperfect process where you can find your perfect match. If you're single and searching, there is no good reason to hide. Give the world access to you.

If you are worried about meeting creepos and a lack of safety, take precautions. Find out if someone has good relationships with his or her exes. Get to know someone over a long period of time. See if the online dating service you're using screens for sex offenders (check with each provider). Run background checks on people before dating them. Start by searching for yourself and see what other people can find out about you. I did. I was clean.

If you're worried about what other people will think, think about all the people waiting to meet you online. Think of the busy people whose paths will never cross with yours otherwise. People who judge you are just expressing their own insecurities. Let that person be skeptical while you go on dates and have the time of your life. If anyone gives you a hard time about making yourself available online, proudly explain you are an attractive person who wants to use every resource available to give people a chance to find you.

Once you find the love of your life online, guess who will be signing up and posting his or her profile? Yes, your critical friend.

Suggestions to Make the Most of Online Dating

- ◆ Make online dating one of many ways to meet people.
- ◆ Change services every few months.
- ◆ Make initial offline visits short and sweet.
- ◆ Use video chatting to screen dates.
- ◆ Past relationships predict future behavior. Ask.
- ◆ Never plan a big first date—small doses work best.
- ◆ Doubt first, trust later.
- ◆ Don't get naked online—people record that stuff.
- ◆ Go after the people you want to meet.

Suggestions for How to Hate Online Dating

- ◆ Plan a first date involving a full day of activities before ever meeting, like you're on a reality show.
- ◆ Take everything personally.
- ◆ Get really pissed off when one person doesn't respond.
- ◆ Make shit up to impress people.
- ◆ Post pictures of a much better-looking person and pretend it's you.
- ◆ Lie about your current relationship status and continue to lie to make sure you can maintain previous lies.
- ◆ Only talk about marriage and asshole exes on the first date.
- ◆ Have sex via webcam before the first date, then get dumped before actually having a real date.

- Make online dating your ONLY way to meet people.
- Build up everyone you meet as THE ONE!

NAKED ADVICE ·············➤

Dear Harlan,
Do not recommend online dating. I've had nothing but miserable experiences online. People are all phonies, liars, and users. I've sworn off online dating. Stop recommending something that sets people up for failure.
    Offline

Dear Offline,
Great letter! I'm going to suggest that YOU take a break from online dating. It's not the right fit for you. In fact, I don't think dating, in general, is the right fit for you. If you get set up and it goes bad, you're just going to swear off getting set up. If you go to a bar and meet someone who vomits on you, you're going to swear off meeting people at bars; if you meet random people and it goes bad, you'll blame random people. The problem is that dating is an imperfect process, but the bigger problem is that you don't have the emotional stamina or skills to handle it. Talk to the millions of people who have found love online—yeah, tell them online dating sucks and doesn't work.

EXCUSE #9: I DON'T DO SETUPS

Having your aunt set you up with her newly divorced cougar friend can be uncomfortable, but interesting (grrrr). Don't let one bad setup ruin one of the oldest and most successful forms of matchmaking for you. Let the people who know and love you the most help you. Considering one in four people met their spouse through a friend or family member (according to research conducted by Match.com), using friends and family to find love is proven to work.

Now that you've trained in your thong and embraced The Universal Rejection Truth of Dating and Relationships, you'll be more open to more ideas. You won't see a setup as setting you up for disaster or an intrusion into your love life. It will be one option among many in your dating arsenal.

Think of getting set up like having a group of agents working on your behalf. They can be in places you can't. They can find out information you might not be comfortable asking. They can set you up with people you might not know or have access to. Just make sure you are at your best or you'll be someone else's date from hell. Get set up, but only if you've embraced The Truth and trained in your thongs. Otherwise, it's a setup for disaster.

Should you get set up and the setup goes bad, try again. If a friend sets you up with someone who has a "good personality," feel free to ask for a picture of this person's personality before going on a date. If the fixer-upper becomes too involved or critical of you, find a different matchmaker. If you have a bad date, don't blame it on the person setting you up or setups. Not all dates will be perfect. Do setups, but do them smartly. Make them short, fast, and at a place where both people can escape quickly. Make sure you see a picture of the person you're meeting—and expect someone to want to see a picture of you (only fair).

Bottom line, it's the oldest and one of the most reliable forms of matchmaking—for good reason. It works.

NAKED ADVICE · · · · · · · · · · · · →

Dear Harlan,
My brother is a great guy, but can't find a girlfriend. I've tried to set him up, but he refuses to go out on dates. He'd rather be single and miserable than go out on a date. He has a good job, but doesn't make much of an effort. What can I do to get him off his butt?
   Sisterly Love

Dear Sisterly Love,
Who would want to date your brother?
   I'm sure he has good qualities, but why would you want to set anyone up with this guy? If he's miserable on his own, he's not going to be fixed by a fix-up. In fact, people who are miserable see fix-ups as a way to reaffirm why they are single and miserable. If you want to help him, encourage him to ask you to set him up when he's ready to not be

*miserable. In fact, show him the people you'd like to set
him up with, but make it a condition that he has to want
to be happy and ready to date. The happier he can get on
his own, the less he'll need you to fix him or fix him up.*

DATE FROM HELL #365

It was a setup. My blind date showed up in a dirty white
tank top, dirty shorts, hair not done, just funky and nasty.
We were meeting at a restaurant—not a barn.

EXCUSE #10: I'M NOT "EXPERIENCED"

One word: practice.

You might not have that much experience, but you will. Don't
hide it or be ashamed. It doesn't mean you're defective. It just
means you haven't been in as many rooms with people and you
keep your pants on. As someone who lacks experience, you probably also lack sexual souvenirs (herpes, genital warts, etc.). Don't
let inexperience cast a cloud over your love life.

It's refreshing. As someone with less experience, you can
make it clear that with the right person, you're willing to try anything. I mean ANYTHING (well, don't say it quite like that). In

fact, you think it would be exciting to be with someone with little experience and a big imagination. Then you can both experience it all together. Or if you find yourself with someone who has more experience, make it clear that you're willing to learn. You can dress up like a student and asked to be taught. Is it getting hot in here?

In the past, you might have been concerned that someone might think you were not desirable because of your lack of experience. You might think someone would see it as a reflection of people not wanting you. But now that you're more comfortable in your "Single and Inexperienced Thong," you can embrace it and let it become a source of strength. If someone finds this to be a problem, that's not the right person to be intimate with.

Anyone who thinks you're not good enough because you aren't experienced is not someone you need to experience.

NAKED ADVICE

Dear Harlan,
This guy I'm dating is the world's worst kisser. He likes to lick my lips like postage stamps and peck like a bird. Then, when he hugs me, he likes to press his chest into my boobs. I don't know where he learned his technique, but I find this weird. I like hanging out with him, but his kissing and other skills need work. What's the best way to approach him without hurting his feelings?
   Dating Pushy Pecker

Dear Dating Pushy Pecker,

He probably thinks you love it all. In fact, he might hydrate before dates to make sure he has an even larger supply of saliva. If you're into this guy, next time you're fully clothed, bring up the topic of what turns you on about him. List a few of his best qualities. Then tell him you'd like to show him how you love being kissed. Teach him. When he pecks, playfully hold his head and show him the way. When he presses into you too hard, move his hand to another part of your body and kiss him deeper. If you want to be playful, put water balloons in your bra—if the balloons break when he hugs you that will show him it's too hard. Actually, that might just get him to hug you tighter—bad idea.

BIGGEST DATING FEAR #903

My partner will want more physically than I'm ready to give at a given time in the relationship. I get hesitant about starting new relationships because I worry about sexual expectations and how it's going to affect the relationship.

STRANGE SEX MOMENT #413

I had a one-night stand with a guy who would not stop talking while having sex with me. But the conversation wasn't about the sex. He was asking me how I was doing in school and then suddenly changed the subject to a friend of mine and if he really was gay and if he had ever had sex with another guy. After a while I said to him, "I don't know, just stop talking." He immediately stopped in mid-hump and said in a very offended tone, "Did you just tell me to stop talking?" Then he rolled over and didn't look at me the rest of the night. I wanted to crawl into a hole and die.

EXCUSE #11: I DON'T WANT TO HURT SOMEONE'S FEELINGS

You are not responsible for other people's feelings.

The other day I was getting in a cab. The driver lifted my suitcase and had terrible body odor. I politely explained that because he had strong body odor and I was a little queasy from my flight, I was going to take another cab. It was uncomfortable, but I figured I'd tell him the truth. I rejected his ride. I gave him permission to have hurt feelings. I was doing him a favor and being honest about the problem. If he was happy with his scent, that was perfectly fine. If his scent is part of his culture, I respect his culture. I just believe in sharing the truth.

Get used to playing the role of rejecter and telling the truth. Rejecting people who want you can suck. It's uncomfortable at times. What doesn't help is keeping secrets, ignoring people, and hoping they'll just go away. That's called rejection by silence and it's one of the cruelest forms of rejection. You can be kind and honest with people and tell them why you're not interested. You can be considerate and caring as you say, "No thank you." Having completed **Step 1** and **Step 2**, you no longer need to be afraid of rejecting people or feel bad for doing it. You are not an asshole for not wanting everyone who wants you. Rather, you are a genuine good-hearted person who might be misunderstood at times. When you say no, you're not an asshole—you're a hero. You're allowing someone an opportunity to find other people who can appreciate his or her best qualities.

As you continue with your experiment, honestly rejecting people will be liberating. How honest you need to be will vary from person to person. Not everyone can handle the truth. But at least you won't pretend to be interested or tiptoe around other people's emotions. You won't play games. You won't avoid them. This new approach will help you build friendships and relationships on an entirely new level. Over time, you'll see that rejecting people will reveal an entirely new side of them. People who are comfortable in their thongs will be able to handle honest feedback. Others will not. Someone who gives you permission to be honest and reject them will prove to be attractive. Embracing rejection is often a sign of strength and confidence. It's why some of the most intense love affairs begin with rejection.

◆ **Warning:** If someone appears to be unstable or dangerous, you don't have to be so honest. Protect yourself and follow your instincts.

NAKED ADVICE ··············►

Dear Harlan,
Is dating dead? I'd like to go on a real date with a real man. Why do men think that hooking up and not calling is the way to a woman's heart? I feel like all the men I meet are little boys expecting me to fall into their laps and do a dance. They want numbers more than they want anything meaningful. Please help me!
   Hungry for a Man

Dear Hungry,
And women always call men back? Women just want dates? They don't ever get drunk and hook up? Why should someone go on a date when they can just hang out and get some? Want to keep dating alive? Be a woman who tells a guy in the clearest terms how to win you over. Don't leave room for misinterpretation. When a man interests you, make it clear what you want. Don't just assume a real man will know what to do. A lot of men don't have real men in their lives to teach them. If a man wants to date you, he'll treat you the way you tell him you need to be treated. He may just need some help learning.

> **MOST HURTFUL THING SOMEONE HAS SAID OR DONE #222**
>
> I thought we were going to get engaged. She broke up with me and then immediately started dating my best friend.

EXCUSE #12: I DON'T LIKE DATING

You don't like dating because you used to suck at it.

Shift your expectations and you will get better. Don't make it about getting married, getting laid, or getting a second date. Don't make it about getting anything. Make it about:

1. Finding out if YOU like someone.
2. Doing something you want to do while finding out if you like someone.

Now that you've embraced The Truth and trained in your thong, you don't need to be validated because you already know you're good enough. This means you can have a date and get to know someone. You can listen and talk. If your goal is to get to know someone, a bad date should be something that rarely happens. You'll like someone or not like someone and move on.

When it comes to planning a date, be active. Find something the person you're dating likes to do. If you can't find something you both enjoy doing on a date, then don't go on a date. That's a bad sign. Always do something you will have fun doing, even if your date turns out to be a big bore. A cool restaurant, a good movie, or an activity that burns calories works (no, not that).

Think of dating as hanging out, but with expectations and clean underwear. When people go on a date, they might expect a hug or kiss at the end of the night or more (that's why you wear nice underwear). People who hang out and hook up don't discuss their expectations. In the past, hanging out was safer than dating because you didn't have to worry about being disappointed. But now, when you go on a date, it's obvious you're interested in being more than friends. Do not be afraid to call it a date—then there won't be any confusion when you lean in to kiss your date while wearing clean underwear.

◆ **Note:** Make an effort. Do your nails (or at least trim them). Take a shower. Plan a night. Get new shoes. Make an effort. Be the best version of you. If the date sucks, at least you'll have new shoes and fine-looking nails.

Ways to Avoid Bad Dates

- ◆ Don't lie, embellish, or post pictures that look like your much better-looking twin. Bait and switch doesn't work.
- ◆ Plan fast first meetings. Research says it takes a man fifteen minutes to determine if he's interested (and thirty seconds to make love).
- ◆ Avoid bar mitzvahs, buffets, and baptisms on first dates with people you barely know. Save family affairs for later.

◆ Always work to be happy outside of a relationship (aka comfy in your spiritual thong). Then you won't be relying on someone else to rescue you from the land of the single and searching.

◆ Avoid going to someone's place or inviting someone to your place for a first date. You can't escape if someone is at your place. Plus, people can be, ahh, dangerous (background checks can help).

NAKED ADVICE ··············▶

Dear Harlan,
I went on a date the other night with a girl who was a setup through mutual friends. The girl showed up ten minutes late. Her hair was up, her nails were chipped, and she looked like she had barely made an effort to be there. I wanted to send a message to all women who are set up on dates—DO YOUR NAILS. Even if you can't afford a manicure, it just makes it look like you don't care. At least take off the polish. Show us you care.
    Bad Date

Dear Bad Date,
And how are your nails? Seriously, please e-mail me: harlan@helpmeharlan.com. I'll post a picture online.
    I agree, it's nice when a date makes an effort. The problem for some dates is that if they make an effort and

*you're not worth the effort, your date will feel like she
wasted her time. Some people don't want to make an effort
because that means getting emotionally invested. And that
can lead to a letdown. Sweats and chipped nails will only
let you down—not her. It's not right—it's just what
happens sometimes. As a rule, anyone going on a date
should make an effort. Polished nails, a shave, clean
clothes, and a little perfume isn't so much to ask. Don't give
up, man. There are beautifully manicured women waiting
to meet you.*

BEST DATE EVER #513

We decided to just watch a video over at my house. It was
really simple and sweet with snacks and blankets. I was
getting drowsy and had slumped against his side. As I
drifted off, I was pulled back by a gentle, soft kiss on my
lips. We cuddled half asleep and he didn't try anything to
get sex. I was won over by his gentleness and his willing-
ness to not move too fast.

EXCUSE #13: I DON'T LIKE PLAYING GAMES

Games aren't fun when you lose. Winning? Now, that's a different story. . . .

Now that you're comfortable in your thong, how you play the game will change. When should you call? What should you say? How should you say it? How long should you wait between texts? Should you use a smiley face emoticon? Should you use an exclamation point? You make the rules now. You do what feels right for you. As you date more, people will think you're the one playing games. If you don't call right away, it won't be because you're trying to be cool—you could be on another date. If you can't go out right away, it might not be because you're playing games—you might be out of town. If you go on a date and don't call someone back for a second date it won't be because you're playing hard to get—you just might not be interested.

As someone who has options and understands how dating works, you can no longer be played as easily. You no longer need to convince yourself that someone who doesn't return your calls is into you. You don't need to wait around wondering why someone isn't texting back. You don't need to creep on Facebook or live in a fantasy world to pass the time. You don't need to wait for people to approach you. You don't need to hold back. You don't need to worry about making mistakes. You don't have to play guessing games. When you have a question, when you need to say something, when something doesn't feel right—you come right out with it.

Remember the 10 percent bullshit that took up 100 percent of your time? No more bullshit for you. You find answers and don't play games.

NAKED ADVICE · · · · · · · · · · · ➤

Dear Harlan,
I've been kind of dating someone for the past few months.
I'm getting tired of his games. He will make plans and
cancel on a regular basis. He'll tell me he's going to call me
and he doesn't. He barely returns my texts. I see him on
Facebook so I know he's around, but he ignores me. When
we do get together, we have an amazing time. It's the time
between that confuses me. I want the guy, but I don't want
the games. Any suggestions?
   Tired of the Games

Dear Tired of the Games,
How about this—change your number, unfriend him, and
find someone else who actually respects you. The first time he
did this you should have told him you won't put up with it.
The second time you should have showed him. Appreciate
that you live in a world of thousands of options. Guys learn
how to treat you based on the limits you set. He knows he can
ignore you, treat you like shit, and still hang out with you. He
plays games because you play with him. Let him play with
himself, and move on to a guy who doesn't want to play you.

BIGGEST MISTAKES SINGLE FRIENDS MAKE #335

Reading too much into each interaction they have with another person. I have friends who analyze absolutely every little detail until they are certain everything said has some hidden meaning and desire behind it. They continue to obsess over it and are crushed when something happens that disproves what they wanted to believe.

EXCUSE #14: I DON'T WANT TO GET HURT

You won't get hurt like you have in the past.

People you've trusted have lied, cheated, betrayed, used, and rejected you. People you barely knew have hurt you. You've been hurt by so many people over the years. Naturally, it's hard to trust again. It's your natural defense. Here's the deal: It won't happen again because everything is different now. How you approach dating and relationships is different. How you see yourself and people you date is different. This book and approach can't keep you from getting hurt again in the future, but it will help you hurt less and heal faster. Here's what's different:

- You are no longer afraid of being single.
- You are no longer afraid of being honest.
- You do not waste your time on bad people.

◆ You are a better listener.

◆ You do not keep your feelings a secret.

◆ You do not stay in relationships because they are safe.

◆ You do not put up with people who treat you poorly.

◆ You do not keep secrets from your partner.

◆ You do not allow anyone to alienate you.

◆ You do not allow others to make you feel less than the best.

◆ You do not allow people to keep secrets from you.

◆ You always surround yourself with people who support you.

◆ You always have a life independent of your partner.

◆ You always know you're good enough.

◆ You always know you have other options.

◆ You always have things that give your life pleasure.

◆ You give people permission to not always want you.

◆ You have the emotional stamina to handle whatever comes your way and move forward with confidence and clarity.

Trust that things are different. If you can't move forward, find a professional who will stand in your corner and help you to learn to trust again. The world is waiting to love you.

NAKED ADVICE ·············➤

Dear Harlan,
I can't get over my first love. It's been a year and I'm still stuck. He was my first everything. The first person I kissed, the first person I loved. We both gave each other our

virginity. He broke up with me and started to date my good friend. She's not my friend anymore and he broke my heart. I can't seem to get over him. Not only have I lost a boyfriend, but I lost a friend. I don't know how someone could hurt me so badly. The craziest part—I miss him so much that I would take him back in a heartbeat. Is that awful? How can I get over him?

    Stuck on My First

Dear Stuck on My First,
I imagine first love is like heroin. Not that I've done heroin, but I imagine it's that intense. That first hit is euphoria and it can never be replicated. First love can also make you irrational (like a drug). TAKING HIM BACK AFTER DATING YOUR FRIEND?!? You must be high. Not only is this guy your first love, he's also your first big CREEP boyfriend! Do NOT confuse first love with being in love. You'll never forget the feelings of first love, but you will love again. Appreciate what you had and that there can only be one first (that's a good thing). Then, move forward and have a second, third, fourth, and fifth. Each one will be different, deeper, and intimate in its own special way. It can be healthier, too. Thank him for being the first and move on.

EXCUSE #15: I DON'T WANT TO COMMIT

It's the same feeling I get at a buffet in Vegas. I'm afraid of missing out on the most delicious dish.

Here's what's changed since you've started reading this book—committing doesn't mean missing out. It means appreciating that you always have options and committing to the best choice for you. When you know you have options, have tasted a wide variety of dishes, and know what you want and how to get it, it's really not hard to commit. When you're looking for a complement and not a crutch, it's not hard to commit. When you're not looking for validation, it's not hard to commit. When you feel good, and find someone who makes you feel even better, it's not hard to commit.

The reasons why people can't commit:

1. Fear of getting hurt
2. Fear of missing out
3. Fear of failing (a lifetime commitment is a long time)

This process can't keep you from getting hurt, but it can help keep you from getting hurt as bad. This process won't allow you to meet everyone, but it will help you meet enough people to know what you're "missing" when you commit (not much). And once you go through this process, you will not be as afraid of failing because success will be defined differently. Committing to wanting it to work will help make it work. Forever is part luck, part nature, and part getting comfortable in your thong(s) and embracing The

Truth. Once you commit to this process and the five steps in this book, it will be easier to commit to someone else and to figure out if they are committed to you.

NAKED ADVICE · · · · · · · · · · · · ·➤

Dear Harlan,

I've been dating a guy on and off for the past few years. He tells me he wants to be with me, but then he seems to go on a mental vacation—not returning texts, not returning calls, etc. When he's back, we totally click. I would say the relationship is complicated. How can I figure out what he wants and make it less complicated?

Complicated

Dear Complicated,

It's not complicated. He either wants to spend time with you or he doesn't.

Know why you're making it complicated? You don't have options. Someone with options would NEVER put up with this bullshit. If you had a thousand guys waiting to be with you and one ignored you, you'd find someone else. YOU NEED OPTIONS. If you can't see it then stop dating. Work to get comfortable in your thong so that you know that you're hot, attractive, and happy without a boyfriend. Don't look for validation from drunk boys who treat you like crap. If a relationship is too hard or too complicated,

it's not right. Do yourself a favor. Send yourself a text, "I
need more options." Then move on and don't look back.

BIGGEST DATING FEAR #901

I'm worried my past relationships will repeat themselves;
therefore, I tend to stonewall a lot of people even if they're
the greatest things on two legs. I'm afraid I won't be able to
keep someone because of my own faults.

EXCUSE #16: I DON'T HAVE TIME

I'll keep this one short (I know you don't have much time).

This is bullshit. We always have time. If Oprah or the president
called and wanted to have dinner with you, you'd make the time.

If *something* is important to you, you'll make the time. If you
are important to someone, that person will find the time. Once
you find the right person, you'll make the time. I love when college students tell me they don't have time to date. I then ask them,
"Do you think you'll have time once you graduate and get a job?
Will life suddenly slow down when you're working full time trying to establish yourself?" Saying you don't have time is just another way of saying you don't want to make the time. Clearly, that
hasn't been working.

The problem is either that you've been hiding behind the "no time" excuse because it's safer or you have a life that's too busy for a relationship. If you genuinely don't have time, find a way to make the time or give up until you have time. But find the time. And do it some time soon.

The good news is now that you've trained in your thong and have embraced The Universal Rejection Truth, dating will take up much less time. So much of your time was spent waiting for someone to find you or dealing with the drama, games, and bullshit. You can now be much more efficient with your time. You can have friends set you up, use online dating services, talk to people faster, share what you want sooner, and spend less time making excuses about time. When a date doesn't work, instead of hating or hiding from everyone (too time-consuming), you'll learn to celebrate, reflect, and move on to the next opportunity (**Step 5** will help).

If you had the time to read this excuse about not having time, you definitely have time to find a relationship.

NAKED ADVICE · · · · · · · · · · · ·▶

> *Dear Harlan,*
> *Why would a guy think it's okay to ask me on a date on Facebook? I know he's a busy guy, but is it asking too much for him to approach me? I don't want to be unreasonable, but as a man, I thought you might be able to explain this to me.*
>   *Facebooker*

Dear Facebooker,
A tweet from your future:

@Girlfriend "Marry me?" #love #wedding #TLF
@Boyfriend "No f'in way" #hugedisappointment
#findanewgirlfriend #breakup

    I know you're irritated, but don't get hung up on it if you like him. If you're interested, send him a reply that says, "Ask me face-to-face and I'll let you know." Should he ask you out face-to-face, make it clear that you're a girl who likes to date face-to-face. Not on Facebook. He might be trying to make it easy for you to say no. At least he's making the first move.

EXCUSE #17: I'M TOO PICKY

Pick up your Picky Thong and please put it on.

    Take a look at yourself in the mirror and pinpoint exactly why you're so picky. What are the qualities someone must possess in order to make the first cut? Why can you only be happy with a partner who has these precise qualities? Which are negotiable? Once you put together your list, explore these three questions:

1. Could you be *this* picky because you are avoiding having to think about the things hanging out of your own thong? Could dating someone who possesses all the qualities you

want to change about yourself make it so you can feel better about you without having to do the work?

2. Could you be *this* picky because you're afraid what friends, family, and strangers will think about you based on the people you date? Could your list of qualities be more about protecting yourself from being judged as opposed to finding someone who can love and encourage you to be your best?

3. Could you be *this* picky because being picky protects you from being vulnerable? If things ever get uncomfortable, being picky means always being able to blame someone else. You are never the problem. Subsequently, you never have to look at yourself in the mirror and see yourself and all your imperfections hanging out of your single and searching thong.

I'm not saying there aren't legitimate reasons to be picky—religion, race, sexual orientation, lifestyle choices, education, and spirituality are just a few. Once you complete **Step 1** and **Step 2,** you'll see yourself and dating differently. You'll also see your list of must-haves differently.

When you embark on your Getting Naked Experiment, pick five must-have qualities. If you can't narrow it to five, conduct your Getting Naked Experiment using your longer list. If you can't find what you want during the course of a year using your long list, get help to make the list more reasonable. You might discover the problem isn't your list or being picky, it's just you.

NAKED ADVICE · · · · · · · · · · · · ➤

> **Dear Harlan,**
>
> My friends tell me I'm too picky. I tell them I don't want to settle. I don't think it's unreasonable to have standards and stay true to them. How can I be picky and not settle?
> **Precise Picker**

Dear Precise Picker,
Here are five "must-haves" I've chosen for you:

1. A pulse
2. A personality (good one or bad one)
3. A job
4. A body as good as yours
5. Someone funnier than you

Or you can go with five of your own. Limit it to five.
Don't look for Mr. Perfect—look for Mr. Interesting. Then date to have a good time. You'll fall in love, discover new qualities that you never knew you wanted in a partner, or discover you're being picky because it's safer than dating. This little experiment is not about them—it's about you. You might be shocked to discover how easy it is to fall in love with someone who is hilarious, adoring, passionate, and three inches shorter than your perfect partner.

BIGGEST MISTAKES SINGLE FRIENDS MAKE #334

Many of my friends are in their early thirties and say they don't want to settle. But they don't realize that not everyone is perfect. One friend stopped dating a guy because "his laughter wasn't contagious." Another because "he was too good of a tipper." My husband is a little too hairy and kind of short. But he has an amazing heart and loves me unconditionally, which is a way bigger deal in the long run than any superficial flaws.

EXCUSE #18: I DON'T DO LONG DISTANCE

But the reunions are spectacular (and very hot).

If you can't find people near you and want to share your life with someone, DO NOT limit yourself. If you live in a community with fewer options, do everything in your power to find people who want to meet you. If you are in a place and time in your life when you can relocate or find someone willing to relocate, go the distance. STOP making excuses. Yes, it can suck at times. But being single and not having someone in your life because you don't like to travel will suck much more.

And really, long-distance relationships aren't like they used to be. With free weekends, texting, sexting (not recommended), video chatting, e-mail, discount airlines, trains, buses, cars, and highways (yes, we now have highways), it's never been easier to feel close. It's not ideal. It's not fun all the time. Good-byes are rough. Hellos are hot. Meeting at a city in the middle is magical. Spending weekends together is wonderful. And having time apart can be comfortable. Especially once you have a life outside your relationship.

If someone is interested in you and that person doesn't live near you, don't be so quick to pass up the opportunity. If you're single, flexible, have a passport, and can legally travel outside state lines without asking a judge for permission, you might want to give it a try. The worst thing that will happen is that you'll fall in love, accumulate a lot of miles, and figure out how you can spend the rest of your life together.

NAKED ADVICE • • • • • • • • • • • ➤

Dear Harlan,
I have a hard time being in long-distance relationships. I've tried them in the past and always get jealous and paranoid that my boyfriend is hooking up with an ex, going to break up with me, or not missing me enough. It gets to the point where it drives me crazy. I've started to see someone and we are going to be apart. I'm not sure how to avoid going down this path again.
   Going the Distance

Dear Going the Distance,
Quick suggestion—date someone closer.

Here's the problem: You're jealous because you think he'll find someone better. You're worried because you're afraid he'll forget about you. You think he'll date his ex because she's there and you're not. Until you can believe you're his best choice, until you want him to have fun without you, and until you trust he's with you because you're NOT his ex—it's never going to work. So, work to be your very best, do things to have fun without a boyfriend, and have a life you love without someone in it. Then you'll be ready to go the distance because you won't be threatened by a boyfriend who loves you and knows how to have fun without you.

GETTING NAKED TIP #555

Draw a one-hundred-mile circle around your hometown and make this your single and searching boundaries. For every year you remain single and searching, add one thousand miles to your search area. Eventually you'll find love (make sure you have a current passport for that date in New Zealand).

EXCUSE #19: I DON'T WANT TO LOSE MY JOB

Unless you're a pimp or a prostitute, sleeping with coworkers may be frowned upon. Yet, dating on the job happens on a regular basis.

And it makes perfect sense.

For the untrained, the office is the perfect place for inappropriate hookups. There are a lot of people in a lot of rooms having a lot of shared experiences. And when people are in rooms having shared experiences, they hook up. Servicing clients on a regular basis makes it easy to service them after hours. A company cocktail party can be the perfect recipe for late-night business meetings in bed. If you're afraid of dating on the job because you're afraid of losing your job, that excuse isn't going to work anymore because you will now be smarter about it.

There are ways to gauge if a coworker is interested without getting fired. You can have lunch, hang out, and make conversation. You can hang out in groups, go to events on the weekend, communicate online, and get to know someone.

If there are rules in place to keep you from dating on the job, you can avoid it until it's too hot to resist. Then you can look for a new job, change departments, or start a business together. Now that you've embraced The Universal Rejection Truth and trained in your thong, a workplace romance can be appropriate. You can build a friendship over time. You can figure out if someone is interested. And you can be smart about it. There's no rush when you're in the same room with the same people, and you're comfortable in your thong.

If you want to date a coworker, keep three things in mind before working it:

1. You must be able to get another job if things go bad.
2. You must give coworkers permission to not want you.
3. You must have other options outside work.

Once you can follow these three guidelines, if you do it with a coworker in the copy room during a company holiday party, it will be beautiful, well thought out, and something that can end in marriage—and a broken copy machine.

NAKED ADVICE · · · · · · · · · · · · · ▶

Dear Harlan,
I'm attracted to a coworker. I'm not sure if I should approach her. The problem is her ex works in the same office. He works under me and I don't want to create friction. I think she might be the one for me. She's expressed serious interest, but I've been reluctant given the politics. Any advice?
     The Boss

Dear The Boss,
Never get on top of the ex-girlfriend of an employee who works under you. Either you need a new job in a new department or this woman is going to need to get a new

job. Even if she gets a new job, you'll have to deal with this issue with your employee. Here's my problem—the world is filled with so many options. You must live in a very small world if this is the best you can do. Put yourself in more rooms with more people who don't work under you, next to you, or on top of you.

◆ **Warning:** If you are looking for a hookup as part of your Getting Naked Experiment, do not look to hook up on the job unless you are planning on getting a new job or getting fired.

Take the Risk

Welcome to **Step 4.**

   If this were a movie, the music would start playing right now (cue the music, please). It's the scene right before the big moment, as you approach your risk. The training montage runs in the background: you training in your thong, facing The Truth, working to get comfortable, running through the streets, getting people in your corner. . . .

   This is the naked moment of truth. It's time to say it, do it, and take action. No matter what happens, you will win. Success isn't measured by results, but rather, by simply taking action. All that matters is that you do something and get used to the feeling of taking risks. **Step 5** will help you filter through the results and enable you to get what you desire. But for now, this step—it's all about taking the risk that leads to love. The music is reaching a crescendo.

   Something is about to happen. . . .

> When I'm in love my bra size goes up a full cup size. When the infatuation ends, my bra size returns to its original size.
>
> *—Juliet, single and searching*

HOW PEOPLE MET THEIR SPOUSE

Via online dating site: 17 percent

Through a friend/family member: 27 percent

Through work/school: 38 percent

Through church/place of worship: 4 percent

Through bars/clubs/other social events: 8 percent

Other: 6 percent

Source: In 2009 and 2010, Match.com engaged research firm
Chadwick Martin Bailey to conduct three studies to provide insights
into America's dating behavior: a survey of recently married people
(Marriage Survey), a survey of people who have used online dating
(Online Dating Survey), and a survey of single people and people in
new committed relationships (General Survey).

HOW TO TAKE YOUR RISK

There is no script. If there were a script, you'd need a script for
every situation for the rest of your life. And that's a big script.
Plus, the lines would always be changing. Then you'd need a full-
time writer. That could get expensive. And it would be strange to
have a writer in bed feeding you lines during intimate conversations. You have the tools to do it yourself.

There are three elements of a Getting Naked risk:

1. **DEFINE YOUR NAKED ROLE: Who are you? What do you want?**

   You are attractive, single, and searching—looking to find someone attractive you can love and who can love you (in your thong). You want to find IT and not have it be a big fortunate accident.

2. **DEFINE YOUR NAKED RISK: What will you do to get what you want?**

   You will put yourself in rooms, talk to people in rooms, and share experiences in rooms. A room is any place where you can have a shared experience (it doesn't have to have walls). You'll ask questions, make observations, and listen to people who interest you. What you say and how you say it will vary based on what you think and feel. You will never forget that you have options and deserve to be loved. You will always give people permission to think freely. You will take all your risks while fully clothed (or in a thong when appropriate) and while totally sober (that's a blood alcohol level under .08 percent). You MUST commit to all five steps in this book and follow them to achieve the results you desire.

3. **NO REGRETS: The only regret is NOT taking a risk.**

   Taking action = success. The ONLY rule: Do not beat yourself up. How you take your risk is based on what you know at that given moment. Never regret following your heart.

◆ **Warning:** *If you're too afraid to take a risk, do not take it. Instead take action and turn to the people and professionals in your corner* *to get help and guidance. You must be comfortable in your risk-taking thongs in order to get the results you desire.*

3,2,1 . . . TAKE YOUR RISK

The rest of **Step 4** breaks down fifteen different risks you may take during your Getting Naked Experiment. These are only a small number of the risks you should consider. If you're already in a relationship, a risk can include facing anything making you uncomfortable in your relationship thong.

> ## GETTING NAKED TIP #162
>
> Do it in a group—when you conduct your Getting Naked Experiment it helps to do it with other people. If everyone in the group is taking the same risks as individuals, you can feel more connected, more confident, and less concerned about what other people are thinking.

RISK #1: DO IT ONLINE

YOUR NAKED ROLE: You're attractive, single and searching, and looking for love via online dating sites. You are taking advantage of one of the most efficient and revolutionary ways to meet other single people. You are putting yourself in the path of opportunity so others can find you and you can find them. You are resourceful and smart—the opposite of desperate. You are giving other single and searching people access to you and allowing yourself to find them.

YOUR NAKED RISK: Put on your *Online Dating Thong* and get comfortable with the uncomfortable that comes with looking for love (or lust) online. Sign up for an online dating service that feels right. Post a profile. Be honest. Don't make shit up. Should you find that you're not interesting, that's a sign you might need to develop more interests. Post a picture. Make sure you look like you. If you think you're too ugly to post a picture, flip back to **Step 2** and train in your thong. When you finish writing your profile, have a friend review it for typos, grammar, and too many references to cats. When you contact people, be thoughtful, write something that shows you read the profile, and make it personal. And don't mention your penis or vagina. Some people will respond sooner, some later, some never. Some of the people you contact may be in relationships, no longer part of the service, or tired of the process. Should you find someone interesting, take it slow. Do not become too infatuated too soon or you'll burn out. Send notes. Video chat. Make sure the person is real. Consider running a background check online. Ask about friendships with exes (if he or she still talks to an ex that's a good sign, sleeping with an ex isn't). Get together in a public place. Provide your own transportation. Make the date fast if you're not familiar with the person. Do not keep the meeting a secret. This way if your date plans on taking you away to Vegas in a suitcase, people will find you. Expect to have an experience. That's it. Be surprised when it's a good one. Change sites if it's not the right fit. Use online dating as one way of taking risks. Don't get burned out.

NO REGRETS: Millions of people meet online and get married. Not allowing people who want to find you would be unfair to yourself and the rest of the world. If you have a bad experience, remember—bad experiences happen offline, too. Don't blame online dating. That would be regrettable.

NAKED LOVE STORIES · · · · · · ➤

A DATE IN EVERY CITY (WELL, AT LEAST FOUR)

I was almost thirty-one years old and I found myself socializing with the same group of women again and again—none of them matches. Then, I had an epiphany. I realized if I didn't step outside my bubble, I'd be in the same room next year and the year after. I was contemplating going to law school. That night, I wrote my online dating profile. I browsed cities I was considering for law school. I figured when I visited, I could find dates to show me around. I thought online dating might feel unnatural—it turned out to be much more natural than bumping into some drunk girl at a bar. I browsed profiles, wrote personalized notes, and tried to make everyone feel special. I'd send between eight and ten e-mails in a sitting. I was prepared for women to crush, insult, and ignore me. When I flew to New York on a forty-eight-hour business trip, I had two dates set up. I asked each date if she could show me around the city. I didn't fall in love, but I made new friends. A few weeks later, I got a note from Lauren:

Hi, I saw you looked at my profile. Looks like you have an interesting background. I know we don't live in the same city, let alone the same state, but I just wanted to say hi.

Lauren was cute, lived close (under five hundred miles away), and reached out to me. I disregarded all the advice about waiting and wrote her back. We built a friendship over the next few months. Finally, I scheduled a trip to see her. Actually, I scheduled a trip to see her and another girl I had been communicating with in the same city. When we met, it was an instant connection. We saw each other the next few days. I did go out to lunch with the other girl, but she didn't stand a chance. After a weekend of great dates, I gave Lauren a kiss before heading home. She said, "I was waiting for that all weekend." A year later, and too many trips to count, we are engaged. I found what I was looking for.

—Jeffrey, engaged to be married

TEACHER TEACHES TEACHER

After making a difficult career change from the business world to teaching, I was consumed with just trying to survive my first year. Every morning, before first period, a female teacher would come into my classroom and rattle off her latest dating exploits from the night before. I was floored by how vibrant her dating life was (I appreciated her as a colleague and a friend, but I couldn't see where all this potential came from). One morning, after my colleague shared her most recent dating anecdote with me, I slipped and said something along the lines of, "I don't know how to ask this, but I'm amazed at your dating life. How in the world are you getting all of these dates?" Without losing a step, she said, "Oh, online dating. You should try it." So I did. It was the most wonderful dating experience I ever had. All my dates were set up for me on this service. All I had to do was show up. The system did a great job of matching me with women I had a lot in common with (far better than I was ever able to, even when I had the time). I think I went out with seven different women and enjoyed all of my dates except one. But, none stood out like my first date with my wife. I could tell by her unassuming and pure nature that she was the one for me. It didn't hurt I was very attracted to her as well. The rest is history. We got married two years later and just had a child this summer.

—Larry, married two years

THE BEST GIFT EVER

Prior to meeting my husband, I was miss Independent International Traveler I'll-Get-Married-When-I'm-Thirty. I was living in China (not attracted to Chinese men . . . sorry!). I had been single for three years and fell for one of those "Are you lonely during the holidays?" ads from a popular online dating service. I was matched with my husband the week between Christmas and New Year's. We met physically for the first time in the airport baggage claim. His first words to me were, "So am I tall enough for you?" Awkward! We've been married for three years. Takeaways: 1. When you know, you know! 2. God bless Skype!

—Elisabeth, married three years

ONLINE TIPS AND SUGGESTIONS TO HELP GET RESULTS

- When responding to a profile for the very first time, try to be literate, avoid physical compliments, use an unusual greeting, bring up specific details from the profile, and be self-effacing (if you're a guy).

- If you're a man posting a picture, consider showing yourself doing something active, look away from the camera, don't be so quick to smile (women like mystery), and if you're a young guy, it's okay to show off your body (but that's a personal preference).

- If you're a woman posting a picture, consider showing yourself doing something active, don't be afraid of the MySpace pose (looking up at the camera gets attention), flirty-faced pictures attract attention, cleavage can help (but helps more with age).

- Pictures taken outdoors don't help younger daters, but help as daters get older.

- You don't need to show your face to get attention, showing a body part or something telling about you can grab people's attention.

SOURCE: http://blog.okcupid.com/index.php/online-dating-advice
-exactly-what-to-say-in-a-first-message/
SOURCE: http://blog.okcupid.com/index.php/the-4-big-myths-of
-profile-pictures/

RISK #2: DO IT BLIND

YOUR NAKED ROLE: You're attractive, single and searching, and looking to get set up through friends, family, coworkers, and acquaintances. You are taking advantage of one of the oldest and most reliable forms of matchmaking. You are using a team approach to explore opportunities. You are resourceful, smart, and efficient. You see the value in having a network of people spanning the globe searching for people you can love and who can love you.

YOUR NAKED RISK: Put on your **_Blind Date Thong_** and get comfortable with the uncomfortable that comes with getting fixed up. Allow yourself to be vulnerable. Prepare for the worst, hope for the best. Make it known to family and friends that you're taking offers. Share with them specific qualities that best describe the type of person you're looking to meet. Creep around your friends' Facebook pictures and ask for introductions when someone tagged in a picture catches your eye (use LinkedIn, Twitter, Tumblr, and other social networks). If a friend doesn't want to set you up, ask why. Don't hate this person for being honest. Instead, if you can't handle the truth, train in your thong.

When you go on blind dates, don't make the dates too long. Always have an escape route. Avoid getting infatuated too soon. Date for fun, not for marriage. Don't talk on the phone too much before the date. The buildup and letdown can cause blind-dater burnout. Meet lots of people. Make an effort each time (shower, don't wear sweats, and show up on time). Go into a setup looking to have an experience and have a decent conversation. Do something that's fun and comfortable. Thank the people who set you up and if it doesn't work out, offer feedback on how to find a better match for you. Be open to any feedback coming from the date via the person who set you up. If someone sets you up with a date from hell, and the person who set you up isn't open to feedback, do not allow that person to set you up again. If the person is open to your suggestions on how to make a better match, offer it and let that person set you up again and again. Repeat the process until you find the love of your life.

NO REGRETS: Make getting set up one way of many ways to connect with potential mates. If you have a bad experience—don't blame the process. All it takes is one blind date to find the love of your life.

NAKED LOVE STORIES ······ ➤

OLD-SCHOOL BLIND DATE

He was a handsome lad walking down the halls of my high school when I first saw him. I barely knew his name, but I didn't forget him. World War II came along; he went into the Air Corps, I worked as a "Government Girl" in Washington, D.C. During those years I met and dated many young men passing through town. No serious connections were made, but I look back on those years as my time of learning about people. The war ended and everyone went back home. My friend arranged a blind date. We were both in our twenties. When my date came to pick me up, there he was, that good-

*looking lad I had admired years ago. He paid lots of attention
to me. We had both grown up. Things in those days weren't
like the movies today with passionate, mouth-exploring
kisses, leading to sweaty copulation. We talked. We had more
dates. We talked some more. He enrolled in college on the GI
Bill; I did the same. After three months he asked me to marry
him. It was on a snowy day in a large public park, when he
said, "We fit together, don't we?" When I agreed, he said, "Do
you suppose we could be married?" It was just what I was
waiting for—I couldn't believe it was happening! I was ready to
live in a tent with him to the end of our days. Fortunately, we
never had to live in that tent. I'm now an eighty-eight-year-old
widow with five beautiful and brilliant children. My husband
was the most interesting man I had ever met; I was so in love
with him, and still am.*

—Arline, married fifty-seven years

SURPRISE BLIND DATE

*I had gotten out of a year-and-a-half relationship about five
months before we met. I was also considering becoming a
Catholic priest. A classmate set us up on a blind date. I told my
date I was moving across the country in a month. Still, we
ended up talking for over three hours. I ignored my "emergency
phone calls" (I had friends call me at points during the date,
just in case it was going horribly). The day after our first date,*

I sent her flowers, telling her what a great time I had. On date two, we had dinner and a movie. She kissed me at the end of the date (she would say that I kissed her, but she definitely kissed me). I proposed in November. We just got married this year!

—Kevin, newlywed

RISK #3: DO IT WITH A FRIEND

YOUR NAKED ROLE: You're attractive, single and searching, and looking for "more" with a friend you already know. You are giving a friend an opportunity of a lifetime—a chance to date you. You are being loyal and honest by not keeping your true feelings a secret. You are immensely generous and very friendly. You trust that no matter what happens, you will be okay because you have done three things to ensure success:

1. You have more than one friend.
2. You have given your friend permission to not share your feelings.
3. You have other options.

YOUR NAKED RISK: Put on your *Friend Who Wants More Thong* and get comfortable with the uncomfortable that comes with sharing your honest feelings with a friend you'd like to date. Once you've done the three things above, make it clear to your friend that you're interested in more than just a friendship. Also, make it clear that you are okay if your feelings aren't reciprocated, but you had to be honest. Make it clear that you value the friendship more than a relationship. If a friend gets weird, acknowledge it. Then make it clear again you are happy just being friends. Ask a friend to give it time. Then, don't be weird. Once you take the risk, appreciate it can take weeks, months, or even years for a friend to want more. A friend might never want more. If a friend gets weird, make it clear that you value the friendship more than a romantic relationship. Prove it by being a loyal friend who encourages a friend to find other partners. After you watch your friend date losers and idiots, bring up your feelings in the distant future—if you still have feelings. You might be in another relationship with someone better and won't want to date your friend. Then your friend can stand at your wedding and think, "I really f'ed up, that could have been me."

NO REGRETS: If a friend isn't interested, move on. That's what friends do. If a friendship ends, it was not a good friendship. No matter what, always leave the door open for a friend to come back into your life just in case the friend regrets not dating you and wants more later.

NAKED LOVE STORIES ········▶

FRIENDLY FRIEND WANTS MORE—AND GETS IT

He was an athlete, resident assistant, and a musician, but kind of a quiet type. I was into volunteering and drama (he thought I was a party girl). Our paths had never crossed until senior year in college. We had the same on-campus job, and

*we discovered that we lived in the same dormitory. We
became very good friends. He would come to me looking for
girl advice. I would share with him my love-life woes. We
would meet for dinner and leave notes on each other's doors.
What started as a friendship became a very big crush for me.
Over winter break, I wrote him a note to say that I missed
him. A few days later, I got a note back, and I danced all
around my kitchen. We returned to school, he invited me to
watch a scary movie in his room, joking that if it got too
scary I could hold his hand. The next day when I awoke,
I found a letter under my dorm room door explaining that he
felt conflicted about our relationship. He wanted to date me,
but he didn't want to lose his best friend—me. I was thrilled.
It's hard to say when our first date was. Was it one of those
many, many "get to know you" dinners that we had before
I knew he was interested in me? Was it the movie? Our first kiss
happened several days later (oh, the anticipation!). We were
talking and I needed to get to work on a paper for my English
seminar. He suggested a kiss before he left. We were on
opposite sides of the room, so there was kind of an awkward but
exciting walk toward each other. The kiss itself was magic. When
it was over, he left. It's tough to write a paper after a first kiss!
He proposed to me on Christmas Eve about twenty months
later. We were opening presents and I said, "This is fun." "How
would you like to have fun with me for the rest of your life?" he
asked. He's made good on his promise. After eighteen years
together, sixteen of marriage, it's still fun—every day.*

—Katie, married sixteen years

IN A MUSICAL

We were auditioning for Singin' in the Rain. *I saw her across the stage waiting for someone to dance with for the tango tryouts. Fate had its way. She was so cute while she fumbled to get the steps right and stomped on my toes a few times. We became close friends, and eventually I let on that I was interested. We dated for two years and are currently taking a break.*

—Austin, just friends again

RISK #4: DO IT ON THE JOB

YOUR NAKED ROLE: You're attractive, single and searching, and looking to connect with a coworker, professional acquaintance, or someone you see in the same office building (or complex). You're working it at work because you share common interests, passions, and employers. You appreciate that the workplace is one of the most common places to find love, but are also aware of not breaking any laws or codes of conduct that can get you fired.

YOUR NAKED RISK: Put on your *Working It at Work Thong* and get comfortable with the uncomfortable that comes with approaching people in your professional circles. Plan on building a friendly working relationship with coworkers, clients, customers, and people at your place of business. Use work-related issues to get to know the people around you. Ask work-related questions. Seek advice. Offer guidance. Borrow a stapler (sexy). Be friendly. Say hello to people you see on a regular basis. Never have lunch alone. Eat with people who interest you. Go for a walk with a coworker. Hang out in the bitter cold and keep a hot smoker company (a minimum of fifteen feet away from the door). Carpool. Get a group together for happy hour after work. Plan a softball, bowling, or athletic team. Create a work band (awkward). Form a professional friendship that extends outside the workplace. Once you're 100 percent sure someone is interested, explore the idea. If a coworker isn't interested, make it clear that you value the professional relationship. Then, move on. If a coworker is interested, take it slowly. Discuss in the clearest terms what it would mean to date and how this would affect your professional relationship with each other and colleagues. If you're breaking any rules, make sure you have other job options or check with a supervisor and get written consent giving you the green light. Oh, and never make love in the copy room (at least during business hours).

NO REGRETS: If taking a risk might mean losing your job, ruining someone's marriage, or losing professional respect, then it's better to wait. That might be something you'd regret.

GETTING NAKED TIP #154

Get a part-time job that will put you in rooms with people on a regular basis. Get paid and get lucky.

NAKED LOVE STORIES · · · · · · ➤

THE GOOD CHINA THEORY

I was very shy growing up. Girls would tell me that I was a great "catch," but never pursue me and just go after other guys. In our mid-twenties, a friend and I came up with "The Good China Theory": When you're single and a "good guy," you're like a piece of good china. Women will come by, oohing and ahhing and saying, "Isn't it wonderful? It's just perfect—what a great dinner we could have with this china." But then when it comes time to eat that night, they leave the china on the shelf and pull out the paper plates. Flash-forward a few years and I'm working at a midsize company. A number of us in our mid- to late twenties become friends and start socializing outside of work. A colleague tells me several of the women at work are interested in me. With a new sense of confidence I actively pursue a couple of women—oddly, none of the ones I had been told were interested in me. I could tell that one I didn't pursue was particularly interested. I was physically attracted to her, but

decided she was more of a friend. One day, a coworker told
her I was aware of her interest, but wasn't interested. I felt
bad and talked with her about it. Surprisingly, she didn't hold
a grudge; she was happy with our friendship. After a lifetime
fearing rejection, to have someone handle my rejection so
maturely was amazing. Over the next few weeks not only did
we remain friends, she gave me advice about other women.
Over the next six months, our friendship deepened. I would
e-mail her throughout the day, share funny stories with her,
and walk across the office to tell her everything first. I
started to develop strong feelings. Then, one weekend night,
while struggling with all of this in my mind, it hit me: "Oh my
God, she's my good china." Once my eyes were opened, I
asked her out the next week. Thankfully, she was still
interested. We've now been married for more than five years
and have two kids. I couldn't imagine spending my life with
anyone else.

—Paul, married five years

WORKING IT DURING HAPPY HOUR

I met him through a coworker. I had seen his name on work
docs and thought it sounded like a dweeby name. Then
I joined coworkers for drinks one night and he was there.
I thought he was really funny and kind of cute but wouldn't
give him my number when he asked (told him to e-mail). He
e-mailed me and I agreed to dinner. When he arrived for

dinner, he had shaved the goatee he'd had the night we met. He was WAY cuter. We continued casual dating, but didn't sleep together for months. After eighteen months and a bunch of breakups, he proposed.

—Vanessa, married five years

WORKING IT AT THE BEACH

I was a lifeguard. He was on a jet ski. They called him a beach rat. He would park his jet ski on the beach and give the lifeguards rides on it. One day, he asked me out. I was very reluctant. I'm a very good girl and he had big tattoos. God forbid I bring home someone with tattoos. What would my parents think? Still, I said yes to a date. He instantly won me over. The first three times I brought him home he wore long-sleeved shirts. We've now been married for twenty-five years.

—Beth, married twenty-five years

WORKING IT AT THE HOSPITAL

We met during my four-week externship where he was working as a medical resident. I asked him two weeks into the rotation what he was doing for the weekend. He said he didn't know, so I asked him to show me around the city. We have been married for almost eight years now, have three amazing little boys (and a dog), and I could not think of a single other person I'd rather be sharing this journey with.

—Karen, married eight years

RISK #5: DO IT AT SCHOOL

YOUR NAKED ROLE: You are attractive, single and searching, and looking for someone in class to date. You share common interests and spend time in the same rooms with the same people on a regular basis. You are giving a classmate an opportunity to learn what it means to date you and have the best relationship of his or her life.

YOUR NAKED RISK: Put on your *Looking for Love at School Thong* and get comfortable with the uncomfortable that comes with approaching a classmate or person on campus. This is a risk that can unfold over time. Sit closer to someone. Ask to share notes. Form study groups. Meet in the library. Grab a meal after class. Make yourself available to this person when he or she needs something (like if they need to borrow a pencil). Give someone easy access to you at all times. Use your relationship in the classroom to extend outside of the classroom. Walk outside of the classroom together to the bus. Talk about class while leaving class. Talk about what someone is wearing (sports teams, Greek letters, T-shirts that tell a story about someone's past, present, or future). Grab something to eat or drink if you're hungry. Invite someone to do something as part of a group later that day or week. Friend your classmate on Facebook. Don't become too obsessed or infatuated— it will just make things weird. Some people will be interested in you. Some will not. As long as you can give someone permission to JUST be a classmate, things will not get uncomfortable—even if you express your interest and get denied, there is nothing to fear if you've trained and embraced The Truth. If someone is interested, make sure you can handle the idea of having your ex in class—just in case things go badly after you learn your classmate is a freak show. If someone isn't interested, appreciate that you've learned something and flirt with a new study buddy.

NO REGRETS: Classroom crushes are a learning experience. Avoid waiting until your high school reunion to make your move. Have class. Do it now.

NAKED LOVE STORIES · · · · · · · ▶

CLOWNING AROUND IN CLASS

I attended one of two universities in the U.S. that have a collegiate circus for students to learn, practice, and perform circus arts. I had never intended to join a circus. I met some guys juggling on the quad, they invited me to a practice, and before long I called home and told my parents I joined a circus. They were relieved I didn't have to drop out to do it. Three years later, I was in charge of the juggling act and had become a talented juggler, clown, and unicyclist. As the new recruits came in, one brown-eyed girl with a larger-than-life smile and dimples caught my attention from across the gym. Everyone wanted to meet this new girl. She tried out and became a tightrope walker and juggler. After about three months of casually getting to know her while juggling, I gained the courage to ask her to dinner. She said yes. We had a remarkable first date that led to a second, and a third. I had fallen for her. We took it slow. It was the first time I felt I was giving in to a relationship unconditionally . . . it felt right. Our relationship was real, despite beginning while she was a tightrope walker and I was a clown, and we juggled our way into each other's hearts. Today, we are happily married (seven years), eleven years after we first met. We have two young children and every day is now a circus.

—Scott, married seven years

SIZZLING STATS CLASS

We met in the spring semester of our sophomore year when she sat down next to me in class. We hit it off from there. We had a Chili's on campus and we went there for lunch a few months after we met. I told her how I felt. That next day we kissed. We have now been married for two years and we named our dog Brackett after the building at Clemson where she sat down next to me.

—Tyler, married two years

RISK #6: DO IT COMMUTING

YOUR NAKED ROLE: You are attractive, single and searching, and on the move. You recognize that you live in a world of endless options and interesting people are crossing your path on a daily basis. You also appreciate that some people are too busy, too shy, or just unavailable. You give people permission to shove headphones in their ears and not talk to you. But you have no problem being the one to initiate conversation and connect.

YOUR NAKED RISK: Put on your *I'm a Hot Commuter Thong* and get comfortable with the uncomfortable that comes with meeting people on planes, trains, shuttles, buses, and public transportation. Look for people who interest you during your daily routine. Do it locally. Do it on the road. When you see someone who catches your eye, start with eye contact or a friendly conversation. While you're strangers, you have something in common. You are both going somewhere, you are in the same city, you are heading in the same direction, and you also both breathe oxygen. Figure out where someone is going and what someone is doing. Ask for directions, even if you know where you're going. Make an observation even if it's not a revelation. Ask what someone is listening to on his headphones. Comment on what she's reading. Say hello. Make it friendly. Be comfortable. And smile. Some people might be surprised to be approached. Some people will be thrilled to meet you. Others will be irritated that you've broken through the I'm-commuting-don't-talk-to-me imaginary wall. Give people permission to be tired, grumpy, and in no mood to meet you. If you have a decent conversation, find a way to stay connected—text, phone, e-mail, Craigslist's Missed Connections. Don't just trust you'll see someone again. Get a first and last name and find that someone outside of the commute (reach out to someone on Facebook, Twitter, Google+, LinkedIn, etc.). If you see someone on a regular basis, don't wait too long to connect. Someone else reading this book will swoop in before you know it.

NO REGRETS: Want to see people who regret not taking the risk during their daily commute? Read the missed connections posted in alternative newspapers and on Craigslist. Make sure the following missed connection from Craigslist will NEVER be you:

MISSED CONNECTION | New York City: I see you at least two times a week in the PATH train station. We usually take the same train from WTC. You get off at Exchange Place. Yesterday (July 22), you wore a red Ralph Lauren dress shirt, tight black-and-white checkered pants, flip-flops, and painted red nails. You are so hot. Maybe one of these days, I will speak to you.

NAKED LOVE STORIES ·······▶

EL IS FOR LOVE

I was on the bus to get to the train (it's called the El in Chicago) to go to work when I saw a guy who happened to catch my eye. When we got on the same train together, I felt compelled to tell him my experience with a soda machine. Why, you ask? Because this is not just any soda machine, it is a touch-screen soda machine with 106 flavors coming from one spout. That was my topic of conversation. His response to my nerdy segue was surprisingly, "Why don't we see this amazing soda machine on Tuesday night?" Very smooth, I thought. We exchanged numbers and a stop later he got off the train. Just like that. Suddenly, the date I had planned for that coming week with another man at a fancy restaurant was not as important as meeting my soon-to-be boyfriend at the soda machine. So began our adventure together; and the adventure goes on nine months later. To be continued . . .

—Rebecca, dating nine months

PICKING UP AT 30,000 FEET

I was recently divorced and working in sales. I was spending a lot of time flying to meet clients and was desperate to get home. I missed the first flight from Dallas and waited at the airport all day. I was finally put in the middle seat, in the last row, on the last plane out. That's when a man sitting in the aisle seat and I started talking. I was not looking for conversation at all. I found out he worked in the food business, and I love to cook. We talked the whole way home. When we landed, he offered me a ride. He had parked at the airport. When I got to my house, we exchanged numbers. We kept in touch for the next month or so. After a couple of failed attempts to get together, I invited him to a party I was hosting. We then dated for the next seven years. We just celebrated our twelve-year anniversary. Oh, I should mention, I found out he was eight years younger than me a month into our relationship. Yeah, I still married him.

—Brenda, married twelve years

RISK #7: DO IT AT A BAR

YOUR NAKED ROLE: You are attractive, single and searching, and thirsty for a connection. You are open to an interesting conversation or a sweaty dance with a stranger as bass vibrates through your body. You are willing to weed through drunken desperate people to find a love connection. You hope to talk to someone long enough to get a phone number or stay in touch.

YOUR NAKED RISK: Put on your *Hanging Out at a Bar Thong* and get comfortable with the uncomfortable that comes with meeting people at bars. Hang out and relax (have a drink if you choose, but keep it within the legal driving limit). Go to a bar with the goal of hanging out with friends, watching a game, or watching people. Make meeting someone secondary. Pick a place that's comfortable and fits your interests (if you don't like loud music, avoid clubs where a Kardashian will be chillin'). Be open to being approached. Be willing to do the approaching. Make eye contact.

Break away from the group (so people can approach you). Approach with purpose. Share an observation. Buy someone a drink. Find out someone's story. Where is someone from? What does someone do during the day? Why is someone at *that* bar? Find out something you don't know just by looking at someone. If the person is attractive, you can mention it, but mention something else, too. You can only talk about someone being so hot for so long. If someone is in a group, mention to the rest of the group that you don't want to interrupt, then interrupt. Or wait until that person breaks away from the group and make a connection. Focus on who YOU like. Focus on who is interesting to YOU. If a conversation is worth continuing, get a number. Call, text, or reach out when it feels right. No games. No rules. Don't be surprised if you get a fake phone number or two. Not everyone is great at dishing out rejection. Some people like attention and getting picked up at bars—but aren't looking for more—like married, engaged, and involved people. Don't vomit, get arrested, or sleep with someone too soon. You will have the opportunity to do all of that later. That's not the goal today.

NO REGRETS: There's little at stake. It's a bar. The only regret is sleeping with drunken people and using your new risk-taking powers for evil. Also, if you do sleep around, the itching, burning, and lifelong sex souvenirs can be regrettable.

GETTING NAKED TIP #155

Some people are not made to hook up or pick up at bars and clubs. If you've never been comfortable meeting drunk people at bars, don't try. Do your risk-taking in other rooms with other people and set yourself up for success.

NAKED LOVE STORIES · · · · · · ·▶

MIDWESTERN GAL PICKS UP NEW YORK BOY AT BAR

I took a road trip to see Notre Dame play Navy. The night before the game, we ended up going to some hole-in-the-wall bar. I should mention—it was crazy hat night. A friend of mine, who historically has much better luck attracting women, approached the classiest, most attractive, and well-assembled girl in the room. Surprisingly, she showed more of an interest in me. I believe her line was, "Hey, we have the same color hair." I thought she was very attractive and her initiation of the whole thing kind of caught me as a pleasant surprise. I'm usually very shy at first. It was a major confidence booster. At the end of the night we exchanged numbers and kept in contact for several weeks. I went back to New York and resisted the notion of having a long-distance relationship.

It had been a challenging winter financially and the travel costs seemed defeating. I decided to date a girl at home (huge mistake) for six months before I realized I was settling for convenience. She wasn't a quarter of that fine Midwestern gal who seemed genuinely determined to be with me. I contacted her in the spring after I was single again. She came to visit me and I then visited her. I soon realized she was worth any inconvenience. I never felt more connected with anybody in my life. Our year anniversary just passed and we still travel to see each other as often as possible. We hope to move closer as soon as we can make it happen. I've never been happier.

—Matt, dating one year

NEVER LEAVE YOUR DATE

I was at a bar for a party on a date with another guy. My date left me alone, chatting, with some women and another guy came over and said, "You look like nice girls, I think we'll talk to you." I replied, "We are nice girls." We then proceeded to talk for what felt like hours. When my date was ready to leave, he told me it was time to go and then walked away. This move allowed the guy to ask for my number (colossal mistake made by the date). I explained that I didn't give my number to men in bars, but that I'd take his. He explained he didn't have a card on him. In a quick and bold move, as I walked out to meet my date, I slapped my card in the hand of my future husband and

walked away. Six months and four days later, we were
engaged. The other guy, I hear, is still pretty mad.

—Courtney, married nine years

LINE DANCING LOVE

Our friends were friends and they got us to talk and tag along
on an outing to a line dancing bar. I thought he looked cute but
out of place in his bubble-gum pink polo shirt at a country-
western bar. He says he thought I was beautiful. We had our first
kiss soon after. Now we are dating and talking about marriage.

—Katie, dating two years

RISK #8: DO IT AT A PARTY

YOUR NAKED ROLE: You are attractive, single and searching,
and ready to meet and mingle. You are friendly, open to talking to
anyone, and interested in having conversations with new people.
You are at a party where you all have someone or something in common. You will talk to someone long enough to get a phone number
and stay in touch.

YOUR NAKED RISK: Put on your *Looking to Meet Someone*
at a Party Thong and get comfortable with the uncomfortable that
comes with making connections in rooms with loud music, little

wieners, and red Solo cups. You can take the risk at weddings, bar mitzvahs, baptisms, friends' gatherings, tailgates, barbecues, or other events. Put yourself in rooms with people looking to have a good time. Be prepared to do the approaching. Sit next to people you don't know. Talk to people in line while getting a drink. Talk to people while in line for the bathroom. Do not talk to them while going to the bathroom (especially standing at urinals). Make new friends. Find out what friends you have in common. Be friendly to everyone. Make it a rule that you will always talk to people who give you *that* feeling. Introduce yourself. Ask questions. Talk about the event. Talk to people who have boyfriends or girlfriends. You never know where or when you'll see someone again. You never know when that person will be single again. You never know if they have single friends. Give people permission to be shy, uninterested, or more interested in appetizers, drinks, and dancing than you. If a conversation is worth continuing, never let it go and think, "That was a good conversation." Make it a rule that you get a number or e-mail address when you feel a connection. If you can't get someone's number, find that person online or track that person down, but don't be scary creepy. Don't wait to be approached—start a conversation, dance with people you don't know, and stand close to the cutest person with a pulse. Make it a rule to never say the words "party in my pants." Turnoff.

NO REGRETS: People come to parties to have a good time. If someone isn't interested in having a good time with you, never let it ruin having a good time with other people. That's regrettable.

GETTING NAKED TIP #156

Have your Getting Naked Experiment group throw parties on a regular basis. Prior to the party, fan out and meet people in other rooms; have everyone in your Getting Naked Group invite these people to the parties. Then get new single people in rooms together and watch nature take over. Create opportunities and fill rooms with single people looking for love.

NAKED LOVE STORIES ········▶

THE CHEESY PUNCHLINE—THEY GOT MARRIED

We met at a party in December 2000. A lot of our friends knew one another, but we hadn't met. I thought he was really cute, but I saw a friend of mine heading toward him. She was notorious for one-night stands, so I elbowed my way over to beat her there. I cracked a few jokes, and he knew the punch line to my favorite one: What kind of cheese isn't yours? Nacho cheese! A mutual friend shared his AIM name with me, so I IM'ed him a few days later with another joke. I wasn't going to pursue it, but I had a little voice that said, This one is special. Don't let him go. We met for bagels during finals and kept in touch via e-mail over break. Our first date was a group date at the start of the semester in January 2001, and we had our first kiss that night up in his dorm room. We were officially "boyfriend and girlfriend" about two weeks later, and said I love you about four months later. I graduated a year before him, so we did long-distance for four years while I finished graduate school and worked my first job. We moved in together in 2006, got engaged, and got married in October 2007. Our son was born in December 2010, exactly ten years after we first met. My husband is my best friend, my rock, my love, my buddy . . . just my everything. Watching him become a father has given me so much joy. Sometimes, I look back at old pictures of us from college and think, Wow. Those kids have a kid. Unreal! I am so lucky.

—Beth, married four years

WEDDING LEADS TO WEDDING

A friend of mine was getting married in New York and I flew to the wedding. I only knew a couple of people. His fiancée had a roommate from college who was still single. They thought it would be cool to hook us up at the wedding. Before the ceremony, we were introduced. We talked for fifteen minutes, but then the wedding started. The rest of the night, she was busy with her college friends dancing and having a good time.

We didn't interact much. At the end of the night, she surprised me by inviting me out with her group of friends. We all went to the bar, including a drunk guy from the wedding. At the bar, he started hitting on her in the most obnoxious way. When I got up to get drinks she came over to the bar to escape. She said, "Want to leave this bar with me?" We walked across the street and sat there for five hours. We had our first kiss that night. The next morning, she flew to the West Coast and I went to the Midwest. The second day home, we talked on the phone and decided one of us needed to get on an airplane in the next two weeks or we shouldn't do this. She came out to see me two weeks later. I went to her two weeks after that. We took turns for the next six months until she took a one-way ticket to be with me for the rest of our lives.

—Roy, married twelve years

NAKED LOVE STORIES ·······▶

PROM LOVE

She asked me to be her prom date. I was in a serious relation-ship at the time. I had never gone out with anyone younger and had never been in a serious relationship with another girl. At first, I resisted. I didn't want to be the couple that made a statement. She wanted to have dinner to discuss it. After our "dinner meeting" about prom, we walked near the restaurant on a bayfront sidewalk. She held my hand and kissed me.

*I went totally nuts over her. I was worried that she saw how
I felt. I didn't want to scare her off! I always thought of myself
more as bisexual, not a lesbian, but I'm now in the best and
most stable relationship of my life. We've been together for
three years and are currently engaged.*

—Dawn, engaged

RISK #9: DO IT WITH A NEIGHBOR

YOUR NAKED ROLE: You are attractive, single and searching,
and looking for some local attraction. You appreciate that being
a friendly neighbor can lead to sharing the same address in the
future. You also know that being friendly can help with watering
plants, walking pets, and getting your packages (and no, that's not
a euphemism).

YOUR NAKED RISK: Put on your *Good Neighbor Thong*
and get comfortable with the uncomfortable that comes with
being a friendly neighbor. Say hi to people you pass during your
daily routine. Start conversations with people you see on a regular
basis. Be friendly in coffee shops, grocery stores, parks, and other
places you live and play. Consider getting involved in local community organizations or activities. Borrow sugar or milk from a
neighbor and bring over a sweet slice for that sweet piece across
the street. Walk a pet. Walk a friend's pet. Go for a walk and pet
someone else's pet. Go for a run. If you're hungry, ask a neighbor
you bump into to grab a bite with you. If you're thirsty, ask some-

one to get a drink with you. If you're looking for someone to run with, ask a running neighbor (but don't chase her). If you're looking for company, ask someone to hang out (see a movie, go to a coffee shop, run to the grocery store). If you have questions about neighborhood events or activities, talk to your most attractive neighbors. Notice what neighbors are wearing. If someone is wearing a jersey every day, it says something (like, WEAR SOMETHING ELSE!!!). It also says that someone loves that sport and team. Shirts with logos, hats, tuxedos, and sequined dresses tell stories. Be friendly, but don't be too friendly with people who don't seem to appreciate your attention. Attend block parties, local events, and hang out at local gathering spots. Try and get outside of your house and allow people access to you. Vary where you go. Make friends, make boyfriends, make girlfriends. Some people will just want to be your friends. Some people will not understand why you're so friendly. When you sense someone is interested in you, express your interest (assuming you're interested). Local love can be convenient and comfortable.

NO REGRETS: Love is down the street, around the corner, or down the hall. Be smart. Be safe. Make sure you don't just blindly trust someone because he or she lives near you. Some neighbors might be waiting for sentencing from the judge or recently released from prison.

◆ **Warning:** *Avoid having sexual hookups with your entire block. Makes for a very awkward (or busy) block party.*

NAKED LOVE STORIES · · · · · · ➤

WALK IN PARK BECOMES WALK DOWN AISLE

I was thirty years old and busy trying to build my career. I was getting tired of the bar scene and wanted to make a change. I lived alone and had a German shepherd at the time. I had just broken up with my last girlfriend a day earlier and wasn't feeling particularly social that morning. When my dog and I got to the park, a black German shepherd and another dog came running up to my dog. The dogs really made the first move. They came up to each other and immediately started to play. While I wasn't feeling particularly social, the owner of the two other dogs was very attractive and wearing a bikini top as our three dogs played. I had to take advantage of this opportunity. We both complimented each other on the beautiful German shepherds. We talked for a while, and this being July third, I invited her to attend a friend's rooftop barbecue with me that night. Our first kiss was later that night at a bar. I knew she was the one when our dogs almost instinctively came to each other as if to introduce the two of us. We are now happily married for seven years with two beautiful children. Yes, I met my beautiful wife at a dog beach.

—John, married seven years

NAKED LOVE STORIES · · · · · · ·➤

RUNNING ROMANCE

I had known my neighbor for a few years. He was a good guy and a sincere kind soul, but I always thought of him as a "friend type." I wanted to go out running one night, and he was concerned about me going out alone, in the dark, late at night, etc. We walked/jogged and talked. At the end, I gave him a hug and went to kiss him on the cheek to say thank you. I missed and kissed him half on the lips, half on the cheek. It was goofy, awkward, and felt so natural. He ended up becoming my best friend and husband. We've been married eleven years.

—Cathy, married eleven years

RISK #10: DO IT ON VACATION

YOUR NAKED ROLE: You are attractive, single and searching, and looking to meet people while relaxing on vacation. You are open and interested in meeting people you may or may not ever see again. You appreciate vacation spots that are filled with single and searching people looking for the same things you want. Bring home a souvenir (not a sex souvenir), a date, or the love of your life.

THE RISK: Put on your *I'm on Vacation Thong* and get comfortable with the uncomfortable that comes with meeting people away from home. This is one of the few risks where you might literally be wearing a thong. If it's a nude beach, you might not even wear a thong. Go to a spot where single people hang out. Consider an all-inclusive resort for single adults. Investigate travel groups for active singles. Vacation in a group with other single friends. When traveling to your destination, take advantage of the brief window of opportunity when electronics need to be turned off and ears are exposed. Start a conversation. Ask where someone is headed. Ask where she's from. Comment on what someone is reading. Ask about gadgets. Talk about the shitty service and excessive baggage fees. Ask someone where to eat in a town you're visiting, where to visit when in their city, or where to spend time between business meetings. Strike up a conversation at baggage claim. Talk in the shuttle. Have a vacation planned that will guarantee an amazing time regardless of who you meet. Try to do things you love to do in a group. Hike, scuba dive, and tour in a group. Be friendly. Be interested. Be approachable. Get to know people from different places. Everyone is from somewhere. Everyone does something. Share your story. Don't just sit there quietly on the plane, beach, or tour bus. Talk to people. If you make a connection, invite someone to hang out while on vacation. Set up a date. Tell someone where you'll be. Find out where that person will be. If you're not able to meet up, or it's awkward, connect once you're back at home. Continue the vacation in your backyard.

NO REGRETS: If someone isn't interested in talking to you, smile, and talk to someone else. Be so damn happy people will wonder, Why is he so damn happy? And of course, be cautious. Some people go on vacation and pretend to be single or someone they're not. Wait to fall in love until after you Google someone's name to see if the guys you've met are really venture capitalists (or just vacation crashers).

SPRING BREAK TURNS INTO BIG BREAK

We went to Padre Island for spring break. We were both attending the same university but had never met prior to the trip. I drove down with a group of girlfriends, one of whom was friends with a guy who would later pique my interest. I would say at least fourteen of us shared one big room (it was college after all) to help keep down the costs. I met him when we were all finally able to check in to the room. We took a ton of crazy pictures (I still have them). We did not hook up on the trip, but the group from the trip met to go out on the Wednesday night after we got back. We kissed that night at a bar near campus. I never tell this part of the story, but we actually slept together that night—which is not something either one of us normally did. It's definitely not the way you picture your first date going with your future husband. A true gentleman, he took me to Arby's for lunch the next day ;). We were dating less than a month when I think we both knew this was special. I wish I could tell you how we knew, but it's something you just kind of know. We got engaged a year later and married a year after that. I'm sure people had bets on how long it would last, but it will be fourteen years in May and he is honestly my favorite person in the world. Some people just get lucky.

—Jessica, married thirteen years and counting

CRUISING INTO A RELATIONSHIP

We were on a cruise. I made eye contact until I finally talked to her. We began hanging out every night, but I had to tell her I had a girlfriend. At the end of the trip we were by ourselves on the top deck, and the time was perfect so I kissed her. It wasn't until six months later or so until we actually began dating. Everything just fell into place.

—Josh, twenty years old and dating

FRENCHING IN THE FRENCH QUARTER

I had just gotten out of a very emotionally unhealthy relation-ship, and my friends wanted to take a girls' trip to New Orleans for Mardi Gras. I was game. The first night we were there was a drunken blur, although I did remember dancing with an army guy. On our last night, some of the people in my group wanted to meet up with another group of friends. As it turns out, my dance partner from the first night was part of that group. So we found each other again in a sea of twenty thousand or

*so partiers. We had a great last night together. We flew home
to our respective cities. I just felt that there was something
there, so I called him three days later and we started our
long-distance relationship. Three years and three moves later
we were married.*

—Susan, married six years

RISK #11: DO IT RELIGIOUSLY

YOUR NAKED ROLE: You are attractive, single and searching,
and looking for a religious experience. You are a spiritual person
and religion is a strong part of your identity. You appreciate that
dating someone who has similar values and comes from a similar
culture can create deeper connections more quickly and more
easily. You are also aware that it can make for a shorter wedding
because you will only need one person to officiate.

YOUR NAKED RISK: Put on your *I'm Single and Spiritual
Thong* and get comfortable with the uncomfortable that comes
with looking for someone who also has faith. Pray you meet
someone while praying. Talk to people when you're done praying (do not interrupt their prayers). Use your church, temple, or
house of worship as a home base. Find ways to hang out in the
same rooms with people of the same faith. Get involved in organizations for young professionals. Sing in the choir. Perform in a
play. Plan a fund-raiser. Look for online dating sites that cater to
a particular religion or culture. Post a profile revealing your core

values and make it clear religion is important to you. Let people who are also religious find you. Consider opening yourself up to people outside of your religion if someone respects your core values. Go to events and activities organized by religious groups and organizations. Help plan the events. Investigate group trips, missions, and adventures that cater to a particular faith. When you see someone who interests you, DO NOT look to marry that person (never on a first date, unless it's an arranged marriage). Look to date him or her. Use holidays, worship, and religious events to connect over time. Invite people to your home for holiday dinners. Go to other people's homes (but get invited, don't just show up). Be a resource for people moving into your community. If you can't find it locally, look to relocate to cities or countries with a bigger population or be willing to travel. Have faith and your prayers will be answered.

NO REGRETS: Listen to a higher power and take the risk. Having G-d (or your higher power) in your corner means never being alone.

NAKED LOVE STORIES · · · · · · ▶

A RELIGIOUS EXPERIENCE ABROAD

Prior to meeting him, I never had a serious relationship. I went on a Birthright trip in Israel. Birthright is a trip for Jewish young people to tour Israel. There were about forty American participants and six Israelis. He was an American and I was one of the Israelis. We did not really talk the first five days of the trip, but clearly noticed each other. In the middle of the trip, we found ourselves talking and laughing in a bar in Jerusalem. During the conversation, I convinced this American boy I barely knew to extend his trip. From that night forward, he and I sat next to each other on the tour bus and hung out during all our free time. I felt the tension building, but nothing romantic happened. After the trip ended, he and I and some other friends traveled around Israel together. A day before he was scheduled to return home, he confessed his feelings for me. Then he kissed me. He told me he liked me from the start, but he did not think I would be interested in him. I was. We kept in touch after he left. We spoke every day on the phone and on Skype. We spent the next year in a long-distance relationship. We visited each other and he met me to travel Europe. The next year, I moved to the U.S. We are now happily living together in the U.S.

—Hadar, happily dating two years

HAYRIDE HANKY-PANKY

Scott was shy and had only one girlfriend prior to me. I had dated several boys but those relationships were often short and sweet. We would see each other at church probably twice a week, then he would sometimes come to my house because his best friend was dating my younger sister. We would often argue when he was there. We would both also hang out with the church youth group every other week or so. First impression . . . Scott thought I was prissy and out of *his league. I thought he was arrogant, strongly opinionated, and was nothing like anyone I had ever dated. I always liked muscular good-looking guys and Scott was a skinny guy with acne. Our first date was on a hayride for the church youth. In the dark maze Scott pulled me in the corner and kissed me.*

—Tracy, married twenty-seven years

RISK #12: DO IT IN A GROUP

YOUR ROLE: You are attractive, single and searching, and participating in a group experience that will help you meet new people. You appreciate that hanging out with groups of people and taking risks as part of a group can put you in new situations with new people. You will use the group dynamic to create one-on-one dynamics with someone special.

YOUR RISK: Put on your ***Single and Doing It in a Group Thong*** and get comfortable with the uncomfortable that comes with meeting people as part of a group. Use strength in numbers to put yourself in the path of people you might not meet otherwise. Invite people to hang out with you and your friends in a group. Encourage friends in your group to meet people in rooms and invite these people to hang out with the group. Get your group and another group to hang out as a bigger group. Get the bigger group to connect with yet another bigger group, watch live music, and call it Lovemepalooza. Go to parties, movies, and events in a group. Play sports in a group (yes, bowling is a sport). Make love as a group (just kidding, wanted to make sure you were still reading). Find three different groups with three different kinds of people. This way you can meet different people from different groups with different interests. If you date people in one group and it doesn't work out, you will have another group of friends and more people to date. When new people join the group, DO NOT JUST TALK TO THE PEOPLE YOU KNOW IN THE GROUP! Make sure you have people in your group who are kind, encouraging, and want you to be happy. When you do meet people who interest you, make sure you can follow up in the future. Never assume you will bump into the same person again. Get a number and go from a group to a couple.

NO REGRETS: Make sure you have more than one group of friends, just in case you date someone in the group and break up. Then you'll always have another group to hang out with.

GETTING NAKED TIP #157

Get five, ten, fifteen, twenty, or fifty-plus naked daters together and make it a group experience. The more people participating, the better the experience will be for everyone involved. Training in your thongs and taking risks as a group will prove to be the ultimate bonding experience.

NAKED LOVE STORIES · · · · · ·➤

BUDDY MAKES MOVE ON OPPONENT'S GIRLFRIEND

He was playing my boyfriend's softball team in intramural sports. He came back to my house with my housemates and was quite the arrogant soul. We were playing euchre against each other and he asked me what it would take to date a woman like me. I told him it was simple, three dozen roses and a bottle of Asti Spumante (sparkling wine). That Thursday, a dozen roses arrived for me with no card. I called and thanked my boyfriend, which then caused a fight (the roses were not from him). That Friday, when I got back to my house there were three dozen roses and a bottle of Asti Spumante. That night we went out. He asked me to marry him. I said no. Six months later I said yes. We have been married twenty-three years.

—Liz, married twenty-three years

BOWLED OVER

We met through mutual friends. We went bowling as a group. We hit it right off, like we had known each other for years. Afterward, she stayed the night at my house . . . nothing happened, we talked and slept. It was not long before she

*moved in, and the rest is history! We are going on twelve
years of being married!*

—**Kevin, married twelve years**

LIKE A TON OF BRICKS

*My new roommate had some of her friends over one night so
I could meet some people. That afternoon I walked into a brick
building (don't walk and text, people!), which left a lovely
scrape across my face and forehead. Apparently this made
me very endearing to one of the visitors, who was infatuated
with me from the minute we met. We talked occasionally over
the next couple of months, and after some heavy flirting he
finally asked me out on a date in November. Within a month,
he knew he loved me and wanted to marry me someday. Less
than a year later he proposed. Oh, and that really important
text that caused me to walk briskly into a brick wall? A friend
was coming into town and had asked what I was doing that
night. Sarcastic me, instead of just saying my roommate was
having a movie night, had just typed, "Meeting my future
husband" and hit send when that wall appeared out of
nowhere.*

—**Michelle, married two years**

ANONYMOUS CONNECTION

I met my partner at a NA (Narcotics Anonymous) meeting. My first impression was WOW. I was immediately physically attracted to her. We both knew within the first month that "this is the one." I've been clean and sober twenty-six years and with my partner for twenty-three years. As the years have gone on, she has identified as transgender, now he is still the one for me!!!

—Juice, committed for twenty-three years

RISK #13: DO IT ADVENTUROUSLY

YOUR NAKED ROLE: You are attractive, single and searching, and looking to meet someone while sweating, climbing, and moving. You want to meet people who love to do the same things you do so you can do them together for the rest of your life—or until the adventure ends.

YOUR NAKED RISK: Put on your *Single and Looking for Adventure Thong* and get comfortable with the uncomfortable that comes with taking risks while being an adventurer. Hike, travel, rappel, climb, bike, boat, swim, dive, dig, run, meditate, or choose your own adventure. Look for opportunities locally and around the world. Invite people to go on adventures with you. Join other people's adventures. When the sweat dries, continue the adventure into the night. Grab some food. Go out for drinks. Listen to music. Hang out. If a fellow adventurer is in a relationship, don't let that stop you from forming a friendship. Most adventurous people have other adventurous friends, many of whom might be single. Then you can go on adventures together and have a group adventure while fully clothed and totally sober (or not clothed if you're part of a nudist adventure camp—is there such a thing?).

NO REGRETS: Do something you love to do while looking for love. If you don't find someone while doing it, trust that you'll still have a worthwhile and memorable adventure with you.

NAKED LOVE STORIES · · · · · · ➤

CUTE GIRL HAS GUY CLIMBING THE WALLS

I had taken a year off from seriously dating when my life was changed forever. I met a girl in a rock-climbing class. I thought she was cute from day one. I never got the nerve up to say anything to her though. When a close friend of mine joined the class, we became two of the more outgoing ones in the class—we had a LOT of fun climbing and making fools of ourselves. Fast-forward to a two-day class trip to go climbing. At dinner after day one, I finally talked to the cute climber. She asked if she could climb with my friend and me the next day. When the next day came, the three of us went climbing. My friend went up first and I was his belayer, which meant I had to control his rope, making sure it remained taught while he climbed. So, if he fell, he wouldn't fall far. Well, the cute climber and I were hitting it off so well that I sort of lost track of my friend's rope. When he kept yelling, "Up-rope!" I finally started doing my job again and pulled his rope so he could finish the climb. When he got to the top of the rocks, he looked at us and said, "What happened?!?" I later explained and he totally understood. At our wedding two and a half years later, he retold that story. When we got back from our trip, I got her phone number and planned on calling her in a few days to set up a date. I didn't want to seem TOO eager. The next day, she e-mailed me asking me out on the date. The rest is history. We've been married for seven years and have our first child on the way.

—Brian, married seven years

MILE-HIGH CLUB

He was her skydiving instructor and she was his student. At first they jumped together. Then solo. He was training to be a photographer and practiced by taking pictures of her during her jumps. When he asked her to lunch, she said yes, thinking it was just to get her pictures. A year later, they got married . . . while skydiving. They said their vows in the air and have been happily married for twenty-six years. My parents took me skydiving for my eighteenth birthday. It was the best experience of my life!

—Sarah, the daughter

RISK #14: DO IT VOLUNTARILY

YOUR NAKED ROLE: You are attractive, single and searching, and looking to give your time to help a cause—and your own cause. You appreciate that people who volunteer share time and a passion. This can lead to more time and passion with someone special.

YOUR NAKED RISK: Put on your *Single and Volunteering Thong* and get comfortable with the uncomfortable that's part of meeting people while serving others. As a volunteer, you already share a connection and common cause with others who volunteer. Use your passion for serving others to get to know other passionate people. Get socially and politically active. Find causes that interest you. Pick ways to be active in organizations. Clean up communities, feed the hungry, plan events, offer services, and do some manual labor. Ask to borrow a hammer or nails when building a house. Talk to someone cute while laying bricks and revitalizing a community. Carry garbage and talk about your dreams when volunteering at a soup kitchen. Meet random people while asking people to sign a petition or register to vote. If you're political, volunteer for a campaign. If you're a survivor, volunteer for a fund-raiser. If you're passionate about a cause because of a personal connection, get involved. Participate in a few different organizations and activities. Invite friends to get involved with you. If you connect with another volunteer or someone you meet while volunteering, make sure you serve yourself and get a name, number, or way to stay in touch. If you find someone isn't interested in being served with kisses, form a friendship. Your new friend can volunteer a friend to be your new perfect partner.

NO REGRETS: Help yourself while helping others. It's a win-win even if you don't get the date.

NAKED LOVE STORIES ·······➤

A LATE-NIGHT HAPPY MEAL

It was just a month into the school year and I had joined the Pride organization. I was handing out cheap ribbons and feathers as part of an AIDS fund-raiser. That's when I saw someone who looked a little shy and awkward. He was thin and had on loose clothing and glasses. He looked out of place. I took it upon myself to talk to him. That's when I spotted a little rainbow keychain on his belt. After our brief encounter, he disappeared. A few weeks passed. One night, after an LGBT event, I walked across town to McDonald's to get some food. Everything else was closed. My plan was to keep my head down, get food, and walk home without interacting with a soul. Guess who I saw waiting in line? A couple of friends from Pride and the mystery man. I could tell by the way he looked at me that he hadn't forgotten me. The four of us hung out in a booth until closing time, then we talked outside until 2:00 A.M. Just before he got into his car, he asked me for my number. We texted over the next few weeks. I invited him to visit my hometown with me. My parents were going to be out of town and I thought it was worth asking. He unexpectedly and enthusiastically accepted my invitation. That started the best year of my life

with my boyfriend. I've started to look at McDonald's and
Happy Meals in a whole new light.

—**Mike, dating one year**

VOLUNTEERING FOR LOVE

I saw her while volunteering at an event. I was immediately
interested. I thought she was so cute! I had noticed her a
couple of days before while we were all doing some prework.
I was sharpening pencils and she was assembling packets.
I saw her at the final event and introduced myself. She looked
kind of frustrated. I just said to her, "By the way, I'm Michael,
but my friends call me Trimm." It was nothing impressive. It
was right before Christmas break, so we both went home.
I found her on Facebook, but we didn't talk much. When we got
back to school, she saw I was online and started talking to me.
I loved talking to her. She cleverly got my number, and we
talked for about a month and a half. I had her over for dinner
one night, and we watched movies until 2:00 A.M. She ended up
kissing me first, because she was tired of waiting for me to! I
love this girl with all my heart and every day is a new, great
adventure with her.

—**Michael, dating fourteen months**

RISK #15: DO IT RANDOMLY

YOUR NAKED ROLE: You are attractive, single and searching, and know that love can pop up in the most random places. You have no problem talking to people who might add something to your life no matter where or when you have that feeling. You are always open and willing to engage.

YOUR NAKED RISK: Put on your *Random Meeting Thong* and get comfortable with the uncomfortable that's part of meeting random people in random places. You will be ready at all times to meet people online, at school, at work, on blind dates, at bars, in groups, at parties, on vacation, during your commute, on adventures, while volunteering, through friends, while going for walks, and while living life. You will put yourself in rooms with people doing the things you love to do. You will talk to them. You will make it easy for them to talk to you. You will be honest with yourself and the people you meet. You know that if you smile at people during your daily routine, say hello to people you meet, make yourself available for conversation, and show a genuine interest in getting to know people—not just having sex with them—you'll meet people in random places. And when it happens, it might appear random to them, but it won't be for you. You know how and why it's happening. You know that you live in a world with endless opportunities to meet interesting, intriguing, and attractive people. You know that getting lucky is more about putting yourself in the path of opportunity and making things happen than waiting. You make things happen. And you can make them happen again and again.

NO REGRETS: You will listen to your heart and let passion guide you. You understand that the greatest risk is not taking one.

THE HIGHWAY OF LOVE

I was driving down the interstate to work one evening. He must've seen me, because he pursued my car, then pulled up by me. He waved, then he signaled to his phone indicating he wanted my number. Of course, being flattered, I gave it to him by holding up my phone number on my fingers. He called me a half an hour later. Then again a week later. From there we pretty much texted every day until we started dating. We've been together for a year and a half. I should mention, I did find out that he had done this before. But I'm the only girl he's seriously dated.

—Stef, dating two years

BAGGAGE CLAIM PICKUP

I met my husband at the Cleveland Airport; I was coming back from a trip. My husband asked me if I needed help with my luggage and I said yes because I wanted to save money on tipping. He asked for my name and number. That was twenty-nine years ago.

—EMC, married twenty-eight years

STARBUCKS STORY

I was at my neighborhood Starbucks having a conversation with one of my clients when I noticed a really cute guy sitting at the table next to me. He was obviously in a business meeting as well and extremely focused on his client. When I got up to throw away my coffee cup I intentionally walked by his table, touched his shoulder, and said, "Have a great meeting." We smiled at each other as I turned to walk away and headed toward my car. Just as I was about to open my car door I felt a wave of energy approaching me. It was him! He was now standing in front of me with a huge grin on his face. "I know this is completely inappropriate," he says, as he gasps for air, "but, I have to know you." He hands me his business card and continues, "Maybe we can grab a coffee or a drink or something." I respond with the only words that I could think: "That's impressive." Within the hour I e-mailed him and gave him my number. Within another hour he called me and set up our first date.

—Lisa, dating one year

FACEBOOK FLIRTING

*I logged in to Facebook looking for people going to my
college. That's when I came across her page. Man, did I think
this girl was cute. So OF COURSE I added her. I started being
cheesy with picture comments here and there. Before I knew
it, we were talking on a daily basis. We Skyped, talked on the
phone, and texted. We're now celebrating our third anniversary.*

—Will, dating three years

BREAKFAST AND A BITCH

*I met her, accidentally, at a restaurant while we were having
breakfast with a mutual friend. It was Julie, Marcia, and me.
Marcia was "interested" in the mutual friend (who was a
notorious player). I thought Marcia was attractive, but very
naïve. I basically ignored her and regaled Julie with my
recent hookup story. We had a good laugh, but I could tell
Marcia was put off. Too bad, I thought. This Marcia girl has
got to lighten up. After breakfast we walked to my car,
where my dog, Sam, was sitting. I let her out to say hello to
Julie. Marcia was impressed by how well behaved and
friendly Sam was. She told me later that she thought, How
can such a bitch have such a nice dog? That was nearly*

twenty-two years ago. Marcia and I have been together ever since.

—Suzanne, committed twenty-two years

More Getting Naked Risks to Consider Taking During Your Experiment (Some Familiar, Some New)

- Step outside your comfort zone.
- Say hi to people during your daily routine.
- Find out if someone is interested in you.
- Let someone know you're interested in him or her.
- Clear up any possible confusion with an ex boyfriend or girlfriend.
- Tell someone how you *really* feel.
- Start a conversation with a stranger.
- Start a conversation with a coworker.
- Share your feelings with a crush.
- Share your feelings with a friend.
- Send an e-mail or Facebook note to someone who interests you.
- Ask a stranger out on a date.
- Ask someone to marry you.
- Find out why someone isn't interested in you.
- Break up.
- Come out.

- ◆ Get set up.
- ◆ Post an online dating profile.
- ◆ Go to an event alone and meet someone.
- ◆ Deal with something hanging out of your thong.
- ◆ Stop cheating.
- ◆ Stop drinking.
- ◆ Stop sleeping around.
- ◆ Demand and/or command respect.
- ◆ Say what you *really* want to say.
- ◆ Do what you *really* want to do.
- ◆ Follow your heart, pursue passion, and never look back.

Celebrate, Reflect, and Repeat

Congratulations!
It happened.

You took a risk. You found a date, hooked up, or found one of the millions of people who won't be interested in you. If you found a date or hooked up, you might be reading this while your new lover sleeps next to you (Note: *Not* a great idea to read a dating book in bed with a new lover). If you didn't find a date or hook up, you're reading this while no one sleeps next to you (a fine time to read a dating book in bed). Whatever happened with your risk, **Step 5** will help you celebrate, work through the results of your risk, and move forward with confidence and clarity. Once you've completed **Step 5,** you will have everything you need to find the love of your life while fully clothed and totally sober.

Congratulations, you're almost there!

Dear Harlan,
I took a risk, and surprisingly, it worked out better than
I could have expected. I finally found the courage to tell a
former coworker that I wanted to hang out with him (I'm
female). He told me he was flattered, but it wouldn't work.
Fearing the worst, I asked why. He then told me he was in
a relationship with a guy. I almost fell over. I thanked him
for letting me know the truth. We then proceeded to have
the best conversation. He doesn't date women—never has.
He was happily surprised by my reaction. I wanted to
thank you. It was hilarious. In fact, I've already moved on
and talked to another guy. I have a date coming up. Also
my new gay best friend and I are going to have coffee. None
of this would have happened if I didn't take the risk.
    Rejected and Loving It

Dear Rejected and Loving It,
Coffee with my new gay friend, $7.50. A night out with
a possible new boyfriend, $75.00. Taking a risk and being
able to handle whatever comes your way for the rest of
your life—priceless. Congratulations!

CELEBRATE: FINDING A DATE OR HOOKING UP

Congrats! Woot! Wa-hoo!

You took a risk and found a date or hooked up—celebrate. Isn't it amazing how easy that was? You're a natural.

You have so many reasons to celebrate. Celebrate that you know how it happened. Celebrate that you did it sober (I'll just assume). Celebrate that you don't have any itching or burning. Hopefully your new love or meaningless sex partner (all sex has meaning) will stick around for a while. If not, you can find others because you have read this book.

If your new relationship sticks, celebrate that you'll be able to make it work on an entirely new level. Celebrate that getting comfortable in your Single and Searching Thong will help you feel more comfortable in all the other thongs you'll wear throughout your relationship, like the Commitment Thong, Getting Engaged Thong, Planning a Wedding Thong, Getting Cold Feet Thong, Losing My Virginity on My Wedding Night Thong, Moving in Together for the First Time Thong, Dealing with My New Crazy In-Laws Thong, Having Too Much Sex Thong, Having a Baby Thong, Having Twins Thong, Having Triplets Thong, Not Having Enough Sex Thong, My Coworker Is Flirting with Me Thong, and the Seven-Year Itchy Thong (probably should wash that). Now you know that whenever you feel uncomfortable in your thong, all you need to do is acknowledge the truth, work to get comfortable with what's hanging out of your thong, and figure out how to turn a sensitive situation into an opportunity to get closer with your partner and fix problems. This will ultimately help you to avoid the dreaded I'm Divorced and Single Again Thong.

That's worth celebrating.

NAKED ADVICE ·············▶

Dear Harlan,
Since I've started doing online dating, I'm finding a lot of women to date. I've never been in this position before. I'm having a hard time picking just one. I don't want to commit because I'm afraid I'll miss out on someone else. Any advice on how to handle my newfound stud status?
    Stud

Dear Stud,
Date them all, but not all at once. Group dates don't work—unless you're on a reality show like The Bachelor (what the hell kind of reality is that?). Enjoy meeting different women and figuring out what you like and don't like. Eventually, you'll get used to having all these options and the novelty will wear off. You'll soon realize being wanted isn't as desirable as being with someone you want. A man can only take so many hot tubs, helicopter rides, and hometown dates before he wants to settle down. Give it time and you'll be ready to hand out that final rose.

CELEBRATE: NOT FINDING A DATE OR HOOKING UP

Congrats! Woot! Wa-hooooooo!

You took a risk and it didn't go as planned. You didn't find a date and didn't find meaningless sex (there is no such thing). Instead you've been rejected or postponed (what happens when someone puts you on a shelf for later). Celebrate that you have new information to help you move forward and take other risks. Be disappointed, but do not get discouraged. People make mistakes the first time around. Steve Jobs got fired from Apple, a company he founded, before being asked to come back.

There is so much to be happy about if you choose to be—I know you might want to smack me in the face for being so damn happy after your risk gone bad, so let me help you see the good in all this:

1. Celebrate that you did something today. You put yourself out there and that's something most of the world can't do.
2. Celebrate that you can take a punch and are still standing. Yes, you now have the emotional stamina to win.
3. Celebrate that you have information you didn't have before taking a risk. This information is golden.
4. Celebrate that you can look at yourself in the mirror and look at the stuff hanging out of your thong.
5. Celebrate that you have people in your corner. Now you always have people to whom you can bitch and moan.

6. Celebrate that you have a life outside of a relationship. You no longer have to obsess, creep, or stalk.

7. Celebrate that you live in reality. Now you don't have to fantasize about the relationship you'll never have.

8. Celebrate that someone knows how you feel and may one day give you what you want.

9. Celebrate that you're not running back to a creepy ex because you're too afraid of being alone (hey, get back here right now . . .).

10. Celebrate that you're one step closer to finding what you want. The more risks you take, the sooner you will be able to get what you want. And that's something to celebrate.

NAKED ADVICE · · · · · · · · · · · ▶

Dear Harlan,
A guy in choir asked me out on a date a few years ago. I wasn't interested and avoided him. I came across him on Facebook and he appears to be single and all grown up. We're now Facebook friends and I'm interested. Would it be weird to bring this up after all these years? How should I do it?
    Second Chance

Dear Second Chance,
Weird would be going to his house in the middle of night, waking him up, setting up a portable stage on his lawn, and doing a Glee-inspired concert. He clearly wants

to have contact with you. Let him. Send him a note and tell him you should hang out and get together for coffee, drinks, or to do a duet. I'm sure he will be thrilled to see you. Or he'll reject you (call it payback). Just call him.

REGRETTABLE SEXUAL MOMENT #88

Drank far too much one night, left the bar with two girls for a . . . well, you know . . . and couldn't perform my tasks . . . too much beer. Chance of a lifetime wasted.

REFLECT: DON'T BE A HATER

Tweeting about an ex's small penis might help you forget your pain for a little while, but it's not going to help you heal. Plus, it's only going to cause the person with the small penis to tweet about your big . . .

If you take a risk and don't get what you want, you might be tempted to be a hater. You might hate yourself for allowing yourself to get hurt. You might hate me for encouraging you to take a risk (no, please don't). You might hate other people for not giving you what you want. You might hate the dating and relationship process because it hurt you. None of this helps you find answers. It just takes up your time and keeps you from focusing on the real problems.

Hating is just a defense mechanism. It keeps the hater from having to look in the mirror and examining his or her role in a relationship. It keeps people from getting close to the hater because the hater is too hostile to approach. Hating keeps the hater from taking more risks and participating in the dating process because the hater hates dating. All these ways of using hate are about haters protecting themselves and casting blame.

But now, having gone through the Getting Naked process, you don't need to be a hater. You don't need to use hating to avoid facing the truth. You don't need to scare people away from you. You don't need to remove yourself from the dating process. You can now see that hateful acts are more about the person performing them than the person they are intended for. When you tweet about someone's small penis it's not about that person's small penis, it's about your big fear of getting hurt or having to look at yourself in your own thong and face your own truth.

Acknowledge when you're hurt, but do not spend too much time being a hater. It will just keep you from healing.

NAKED ADVICE ··············▷

Dear Harlan,
I hate men. You are all pigs. I've been cheated on twice. The other times I've been hurt by men who seemingly only want to sleep with me. Once a man has sex with me, he dumps me. Why do all men hurt me?
    Hater

Dear Hater,

Come on! Just some of us are pigs. . . .

I have a friend who isn't a pig. I also have five Facebook friends who are not pigs. That makes six. And I'm not a pig. Now, seven, that's seven total non-pigs. Now that this is clear, I'm going to tell you something as a man, not a pig. You might have a role in this. You might attract pigs. You might make it easy for pigs. Instead of hating all men, figure out your role in this. You might be meeting the wrong men in the wrong places. You might be trusting too quickly, hanging on too tightly when there are bad signs, or having sex too soon. Go slower. Meet men in different places. Wait a long time before having sex. Look for a man who has exes who don't hate him (men with exes who don't hate them tend to be good guys). But blaming all men for all the bad in your life is not healthy—some of us aren't pigs. At least seven of us . . .

BIGGEST MISTAKES SINGLE FRIENDS MAKE #321

They expect the other person to be a mind reader. We expect our partners to just know what we want, why we're feeling a certain way—everything. It's not fair to either partner. Unless someone expresses it, there's just no way to know it.

REFLECT: DON'T BE A HIDER

You might want to drink a couple of bottles of Chianti, eat a few pints of ice cream, and have sex with a friend to hide from the pain, but don't. Instead, have a glass of wine, a serving of ice cream, and spend a romantic evening making wild love to yourself (batteries are not included in this book).

If things go bad, your knee-jerk reaction might be to go into hiding. It's what so many of us learn to do. You might want to hide from yourself, other people, or dating and relationships. Recognize this is just you trying to protect yourself from facing The Universal Rejection Truth and the ugly things hanging out of your thong. You no longer need to go into hiding.

You no longer need to hide in crappy relationships by having meaningless sex (see, it does have meaning), by using drugs or alcohol, by hating and creating distractions, by insulating yourself with friends, by overeating, by overindulging, by using technology, or by doing anything and everything you can to avoid facing The Truth.

When you're comfortable in your thongs and can accept The Universal Rejection Truth, you'll see hiding as just another way to keep you from getting hurt, feeling vulnerable, or facing the uncomfortable truth. It's running away from yourself. It's running away from people who will make you think about uncomfortable parts of yourself. Now that you've trained, you no longer need to hide because none of this hurts as much. You no longer have a reason to hide.

◆ **Warning:** When you hurt and want to hide, or give up, put on your Single and Rejected Thong and reflect. Work through the three obstacles in the next sections and avoid going into hiding.

NAKED ADVICE ·············▶

Dear Harlan,
I've been dating the same guy for the past three years. He's mentioned proposing and we've started to look at rings. At times, I think the relationship is more about comfort than passion. I have to admit, I like having someone to go out with and not worrying about being alone. I'm not ready to get married, but I'm not ready to be single. How can I avoid having him pop the question?
   Dead-End Dater

Dear Dead-End Dater,
You might want to pop the question, "Want to date other people?"
   Hiding in a relationship because you don't want to be single is selfish. It keeps him from meeting women who can love him and it keeps you from meeting other guys you could love. Do everyone a favor—if you need a companion, get a dog. See how it feels to be single. If your man finds a better fit during your brief time apart, be happy for him.

There are plenty of men with whom you can be comfortable.
You all deserve the best (including the dog).

MOST HURTFUL THING SOMEONE HAS SAID OR DONE #444

He just kind of disappeared. I didn't hear anything from him for several months and he didn't answer my e-mails. Then I got an e-mail from him months later asking if I had fallen off the face of the earth. When HE was the one who wasn't contacting ME.

REFLECT: THE THREE FORMS OF ADVERSITY

Before slipping into your Risk-Taking Thong and reflecting on the risk(s) you've taken in **Step 4,** you need to be aware of the three forms of adversity you will encounter should a risk not go as planned. Being aware and being able to work through each form of adversity is essential to finding answers and ultimately getting the results you desire.

The Three Forms of Adversity You May Face

1. **Self-rejection**

    The act of *rejecting oneself* before ever allowing others the opportunity to do so.

2. **Rejection by circumstance**

    Your desired result is *not* achieved due to a circumstance that *may or may not* be directly related to you.

3. **Raw rejection**

    Your desired result is *NOT* achieved due to a circumstance that is *directly* related to you. The circumstance is a factor that you cannot change or choose not to change because changing would mean compromising a fundamental part of your character.

REFLECT: UMM, IS IT ME?

Should your risk not have gone as planned, you will have to work through the first form of adversity.

SELF-REJECTION

Self-rejection is the act of rejecting yourself before ever allowing anyone else to reject you. You may have trained in **Step 2,** but your training could be incomplete. There may still be things hanging out of your thong. You might not have truly been taking and committing to taking your risk. People in a state of self-rejection are more comfortable rejecting themselves because it's safer. When you reject yourself, you know what's wrong with you. When someone else rejects you, it's not quite clear why someone doesn't want you. And that's too painful.

Make sure your biggest problem is NOT you. Ask yourself the following questions to be sure you've properly trained and are not your own worst enemy during your Getting Naked Experiment:

1. *Is this the very best version of me?*
   You will only feel like the best version of you if you're comfortable in your thongs. This means always working to love what you can't change and changing what you don't love. If you're not there yet, keep training.

2. *Did I make my best effort?*
   Don't bullshit yourself. Is something still holding you back? What is it? How can you train to get beyond it? If you're unsure what's holding you back, turn to the people in your corner and keep training.

3. *Did I truly think I could be successful taking this risk?*
   If you didn't think it could happen, then you are your own worst enemy. You must believe you can be successful before taking future risks. Keep training and turn to the people in your corner for guidance.

Once you're at your personal best and make your best effort, you will be able to move forward.

NAKED ADVICE ············▶

Dear Harlan,
Whenever I talk to a girl, I have this sinking feeling that as soon as I walk away she's thinking bad things about me, like, Who does that guy think he is talking to me? It's caused me to stop talking to women because I get it in my head that I'm being annoying and irritating. Any advice to get over this?
   Accidentally Annoying

Dear Accidentally Annoying,
The problem could be that you're using a pickup line about your pants magically disappearing—never a good idea.
   The bigger problem is that you're rejecting yourself before ever allowing anyone to reject you. You are your own worst enemy. Before approaching more women, work on a new approach to dating. Take time to get comfortable in your thong. Work to get incredibly attractive without dating anyone. Train physically, emotionally, and spiritually. Do everything you can so that you know you're hot enough. Over time, you'll naturally approach women with a new approach. Instead of assuming the worst, you'll assume the best because you're at your best.

REASON WHY I'M SINGLE #227

Sometimes I think I must just be ugly or give off the impression that I don't want people to approach me. But then again, I think I'm really not that bad looking and I try my best to come off as friendly, fun, and likable. Obviously that isn't working. So, I really have no idea why I'm single. I don't even understand it.

REFLECT: UMM, IS IT YOU?

Once you've examined your role in the risk, it's time to turn your attention to the people (or person) not giving you what you want. This means working through the second form of adversity:

REJECTION BY CIRCUMSTANCE

The circumstance causing you to get an undesirable result might have NOTHING to do with you or EVERYTHING to do with you.

For example, the person you desire might be in another relationship, emotionally unavailable, dealing with personal issues, gay, lesbian, bisexual, or going to prison in a few weeks (that could be problematic). These are all circumstances that have NOTHING to do with you, your personality, or your appearance. Until you know the circumstances behind the rejection, never assume the problem is you.

Then again, the circumstance may have everything to do with you. Someone might not want you for reasons you may or may not be able to or want to change. It may be your religion, your race, your job, your height . . . the list goes on and on. Once you've trained and embraced The Universal Rejection Truth of Dating and Relationships, finding out the circumstance behind the rejection will help you understand why the risk didn't go as planned and how to move forward. For example, if the circumstance is your approach, you can change your approach or approach someone else. If the circumstance is your appearance, you can possibly change your appearance or love what you can't change and move on. If the circumstance has nothing to do with you, figure out if the outcome you desire may be possible once the circumstance changes (i.e., someone is just out of a relationship and needs time to heal).

Now, when someone you desire isn't interested, don't beat yourself up or wonder why—find out the circumstance. Ask the person not giving you what you want, "Why?" If that person hesitates, forget it and move on. If he or she gives you a reason, accept it—even if it's painful to hear. Do not hate or hide. Be grateful. Either make changes (if it will change the outcome and you're not compromising your values) or move on to the next risk. If you hear the same reason three times from three different people, chances are the feedback is valid and true. For example, if three women tell you they don't date married men, then being married might be hurting your chances of getting a date.

REMINDER: When you live in a world of options, embrace The Truth and train in your thongs. The Truth will no longer hurt as much. It will just make you think and force you to look at yourself in your thong and change what you don't love or work to love what you can't change.

Dear Harlan,
I went on what was probably the best first date ever.
We laughed all night, held hands, and kissed. It wasn't
just a regular kiss. It was a knee-buckling-need-more-
don't-want-to-take-my-lips-away-from-him kind of kiss. It's
been a week and no call! I called him a couple of days ago,
but still, nothing! What the F! I've gone through everything
that happened and what I could have said or done to cause
this. Still, I can't imagine what I did wrong. He's leaving me
hanging. Advice, man? Looking for a guy's point of view.
  Hanging

Dear Hanging,
  A guy who doesn't call a girl:

1. *Doesn't want to call you because he's not interested (i.e.,*
   dating someone else, trying to be cool, gay, or any other
   reason that has nothing to do with you until you know
   otherwise).
2. *Is in the hospital, in jail, or dead and can't call.*
3. *Lost your information and really wants to get in touch.*

Considering you called and left your number, he could be a knee-buckling-kissing-stuck-on-his-ex-while-kissing-you-and-pretending-you're-her kind of guy. Or he's sick, in jail, dead, or not interested. When he wants to find you he can call, e-mail, text, tweet, Facebook, knock on your door, send a letter, send flowers, send dinner, and ask you on another date. Until then, find other dates and hope he gets out of the hospital or is released from prison soon.

MOST HURTFUL THING SOMEONE HAS SAID OR DONE #450

I was moving cross-country to live with my boyfriend. We were traveling to Burning Man, a huge gathering in the desert. We picked up my good friend along the way. Ends up, she shared a tent with us. In the middle of the night, she hooked up with my boyfriend on the same air mattress we all shared. What a bitch!

REFLECT: IT IS WHAT IT IS (AND IT'S CALLED THE UNIVERSAL REJECTION TRUTH)

There's a chance someone you want will NEVER want you. And the reason will have EVERYTHING to do with you. When someone doesn't want you, and will never want you, you will face the third and most debilitating form of adversity:

RAW REJECTION

No matter what you say, no matter what you do, someone you want will NEVER want you because you are you. That's raw rejection. If you can change yourself to get someone to like you, changing would mean compromising a fundamental part of your identity. The problem could be your religion, faith, sexual history, appearance, personality, or passion. For single and searching people stuck in rejection denial, it can knock them out. Facing raw rejection even once can sideline the untrained for life. It can turn them into permanent haters or hiders. Raw rejection can be that dangerous.

But for you, raw rejection will no longer be devastating. It just confirms what you already know—not everyone will want you.

Big deal. Right? You were over this in **Step 1.**

Being comfortable in your thongs, embracing The Truth, and living in a world of options takes all the punch out of raw rejection. If someone isn't interested, you move on to the next opportunity. It's not that you don't care; you just care to spend your time taking other risks so you can get what you want—and you truly understand what you want. You can only control so much. The rest is what it is. In fact, the expression "It is what it is" is just the name we give The Universal Rejection Truth. The difference between you and the rest of the world is that you can accept and truly understand what "it is."

NAKED ADVICE · · · · · · · · · · · · ·▶

Dear Harlan,
I'm a black woman who is interested in dating white men.
I know not all white men are open to this. How do I ap-
proach a white man who has never dated a black woman?
   Beautiful Black Woman

Dear BBW,
As a white man, I can speak on behalf of all white men of the
world: If you put on your beautiful black thong and approach
us, most of us will forget the color of your skin (Note: Wear
clothing over your thong, unless you are approaching white
men on a hot beach). The ones who have a problem with
your skin tone can get out of the way and let the rest of the
white men experience your beautiful black magic. Give all
white men permission to love you. Give them all permission
to never know what they're missing. Form friendships with
white men so they can understand exactly what it means to
get to know a beautiful black woman. Once they go black,
they'll never go back. Or is that just a rumor?

**MOST HURTFUL THING SOMEONE HAS SAID
OR DONE** #455

"You are so fucking stupid, I never want to see you again."
An ex-boyfriend via a text message.

REFLECT: TURN TO THE PEOPLE
IN YOUR CORNER

As you work through each risk and navigate through the three
forms of adversity, you will need to lean on people who can offer
guidance and provide perspective. These are the people in your
corner. Use them. Avoid getting defensive or making excuses. Don't
get pissed off. Listen to their objective opinions. When you get the
same feedback from three different people in your corner—trust
that it's true (unless you're paying the people in your corner millions of dollars and they depend on you for all their income—then
the truth will be too hard for them to share because it may get
them fired). If everyone has a different opinion, listen to everyone's thoughts, but take the ones you like best (sounds fair). **Make
sure the people in your corner want you to succeed and want
you to be happy.**

- NEVER let someone you're dating keep you from seeking
  advice and guidance from the people in your corner.

Controlling partners and abusers might not want you to turn to people in your corner. Why? They're going to tell you the truth. When a partner is threatened by your loving family and friends in your corner, it's a red flag.

◆ If it takes too long to get the results you desire, turn to professionals and/or other experts who can help you. Not all friends and family are equipped to help you find answers. A lot of them are struggling with the same issues. Having a therapist, psychologist, or counselor in your corner will help you be more open to feedback. It's the difference between your mom, dad, sibling, or best friend telling you the truth versus a licensed professional. Therapists don't bring up your issues and call you out at family dinners.

NAKED ADVICE • • • • • • • • • • • ➤

Dear Harlan,
A girl I've been dating is torn between another guy and me. She says she's in love with two different people, but doesn't know which one of us to date. There are parts of both of us she loves. I find this very upsetting to say the least. We have the best time. I can see spending my life with her. I don't want to let her go. How can I convince her to choose me?
   Fighting

Dear Fighting,
Give her the best kiss of her life. Tell her you'd love to date
her exclusively. Then ask her to figure it out, but to not call,
text, or get in touch until she's figured it out. Let her know
it's too hard for you. No creeping, texting, or mind games.
Stay busy doing the things you love to do. If you don't have
anything you love to do, find something. Get set up. Try
dating online. Date other people. I'm not suggesting you hide
your feelings or not fight for her, but you can't convince
someone to love you. If she doesn't figure it out now, she'll
always be looking over her shoulder wondering if she's with
the best guy. Save yourself couples therapy, a divorce, and
custody battles. Give her time and space to figure out that
you're the best choice—only she can convince herself.

REASON WHY I'M SINGLE #215

In an effort to support my own health and well-being I've
decided to stay single for a while. This has helped me learn
more about who I am as an individual. It's better for me to
be single than to waste time with a loser when the real
thing could come along.

REFLECT: TAKE TIME TO RECOUP

Once you've celebrated and reflected, take a break and give yourself time to recoup. Give your mind and body time to heal. Clear your head. Cleanse your mind. Hang out with friends. Do something you love to do. Spoil yourself. Just take time to take care of you.

Do not bounce around from one relationship to another. It won't give you time to reflect. Spend time thinking. Spend time breathing. Spend time gaining perspective so you can move forward with clarity, learn from the past, and not repeat old patterns. The beauty of having trained in your spiritual thong is that you ALWAYS have a life to return to following a risk or romantic relationship. And the beauty of always having people in your corner is that you always have people to lean on and hang out with. Enjoy the break. Savor it.

(imagine ocean sounds or play via *Getting Naked* audio book)

NAKED ADVICE · · · · · · · · · · · · ·➤

Dear Harlan,
I just got out of an emotionally abusive relationship.
I found out my boyfriend was cheating on me for most of
our relationship. I've started dating again, but seem to
sabotage the relationships before they get to a place where
I need to trust a guy again. I can't handle getting hurt like

I did in the past. How can I open up and let someone in when I'm so scared of being vulnerable?
   Stuck Behind Walls

Dear Stuck Behind Walls,
It's like getting mugged in a safe neighborhood (happened to me). You feel violated, vulnerable, and scared it will happen again. It's hard to walk around with that same sense of safety ever again—you're not the same person.

Stop dating for a while. Put a space between you and the pain. Then, after some distance, look back and see what happened. Examine his role. Look at your role. Figure out what you can do to be safely vulnerable. Spend time with friends. Go on vacation. Do things you love to do on your own. Rebuild your sense of self. Consider building friendships with men before dating them. Get to know their pasts before trusting them in the future. Also, talk to a therapist who can help you make sense of the past and stand in your corner in the future. Before you date again, you must understand what happened in the past so you can make changes and open up again in the future—otherwise, you'll get stuck hating men or hiding from them.

REPEAT: TAKE THE SAME RISK AGAIN—OR FIND A NEW ONE

Once you're ready to take another risk, there are two questions you'll want to ask yourself before moving forward:

1. Do I want to take the same risk again with the same person?

2. Do I need to take a new risk with a new person?

If you take the same risk with the same person, make sure something has changed. Once you work through the three forms of adversity, you'll have an idea of what must change in order to get the results you desire. For example, if you feel you could have done something better or differently the first time around, try the same risk again and make some changes. If you discovered the circumstance behind the rejection was something that you could change over time, change it and then try again. If you discovered the circumstance is something that will NEVER change (because you can't change it or aren't willing to compromise a fundamental part of you or your character), then don't take that risk again. Move on to the thousands of other options available to you and don't look back. While you change or wait for people to change, NEVER stop moving forward. NEVER stand around waiting. Always keep moving forward and putting yourself in more rooms with more people.

Should you decide to take an entirely new risk with an entirely new person, start by defining the risk you want to take and your role. Next, put on your Risk-Taking Thong and look at what makes you uncomfortable about the risk. Once you get comfortable with the uncomfortable, there will be no room to make excuses. Then it will be time to take the risk. Following each risk, celebrate, reflect, and repeat the process until you get your desired results.

Pretty simple stuff, right?

Once you get in a groove and get comfortable in your Risk-Taking Thong, your focus will shift. You'll become acute at spotting people in rejection denial who are uncomfortable in their thongs. You'll pick up on the excuses people make to protect themselves. You'll be more interested why someone is attacking you than the fact that you're being attacked. You'll see why most people let the 10 percent bullshit consume 100 percent of their time.

As for you, you'll find it easy to sidestep drama, not get caught up in games, and always have perspective. Life will be less about being validated and more about exploring options. You'll find new ways to spend time with yourself and people who give your life meaning. The entire dating process will be more relaxing and enjoyable. And the best part—you can handle it all while fully clothed and totally sober.

NAKED ADVICE · · · · · · · · · · · ·▶

> *Dear Harlan,*
> *All my friends are getting married and engaged to their*
> *college boyfriends and I'm the last single girl. I'm starting*
> *to feel this sense of panic because I'm not with anyone. I'm*

getting swept up in a tide of weddings and feel I'm about to miss the boat. Have any advice to calm my fear and make sure I don't get stranded?
    Drifting into Panic

Dear Drifting into Panic,
Being the last single girl has its perks. This would make you the only single girl at your friends' weddings. Which would make you one extremely sought-after girl by all the single men at the weddings. If you go to enough weddings, you'll find your own man and then have a wedding of your own. By the time your wedding comes around, some of your recently married friends might be single again. Then they will be able to find their second husbands at your wedding.

NAKED FINAL EXAM

You've now completed the five steps. Congratulations. Your world will never be the same again. To prove it, let's look back at the five questions from the first page of the book.

QUESTION: When you see someone who gives you *that* feeling, what do you do?

THE ANSWER: You say what you're thinking. You listen to what people have to say. You never avoid an opportunity to take a risk because you're afraid of getting rejected. The only reason you won't take a risk is because it's too dangerous (you will get beat up, get fired, or arrested), or it's not the right decision for you at that time.

NEXT QUESTION: What if you knew with absolute certainty that, at all times, you had thousands of people who wanted to hook up with you, have sex with you, and do everything you wanted to do in a consensual way? Would you ever hook up or sleep with someone who might be in a relationship, married, deceitful, or hiding a secret sex souvenir that will leave you itching or burning when the sex ends?

THE ANSWER: No way (at least not sober). In fact, when sex is available, you don't *need* to have it. You can wait. You can talk about it. You can find out someone's first and last names. You can talk about someone's sexual past and what having sex means to the future of your relationship. You can talk about sex on Saturday night, get tested for chlamydia on Wednesday, and have sex the next week after the results come back. Or, you can wait until marriage (yes, some people still do that). There's no rush.

NEXT QUESTION: If you knew that, at all times, you had thousands of people who wanted to date you, love you, and treat you the way you deserve to be treated, would you ever put up with one person who treated you like crap?

THE ANSWER: Never. And you NEVER will again.

NEXT QUESTION: Why do so many people put up with so much crap in relationships?

THE ANSWER: They don't know they live in a world of options, don't feel good enough in their thongs to explore their options, and can't handle it when someone they like doesn't like them back. That's not you. You alway have options, feel good enough to explore them, and give people permission to miss out on your hotness. You know dating is an imperfect process. All you have to do is be your best. When you're at your best, you know you'll find your best choice.

LAST QUESTION: What if you knew that at all times you lived in a world of endless options, could take emotional risks at will, and could find sex, love, and passion simply by embracing a secret truth, getting comfortable in your thong, and always expressing what you felt?

THE ANSWER: Now you know. You feel more hopeful, excited, and ready to find the love of your life.

PART III

◀ ·························· ▶

The Getting Naked Experiment

Naked Reminder: Once you complete Part III, you're invited to visit www.gettingnaked experiment.com to begin your experiment.

Dear Harlan,
How do you know this Getting Naked approach really
works?
    Everyone Reading This Book

Dear Everyone Reading This Book,
Start with my wife. Then, ask the other people who have
taken risks and found love. Then try it. Then ask your new
boyfriend, girlfriend, husband, wife, or life partner.

My Getting Naked Experiment
Part One

I've been waiting to share this story with you the entire book. I didn't want to share it too soon. But now, after reading the first two parts of this book, you might be more interested in how this approach and Getting Naked Experiment came to be. Before getting into the details, I'd like to start with my own personal dating, relationship, and sexual history (a very short story):

It all started in kindergarten. It was a playdate at my place. The same place I shared with my parents. After some milk and cookies, Amy and I made our way into the basement. We climbed on top of the beanbags and had our first kiss. It was on the cheek and innocent enough. Minutes later, her mom honked the horn and our playdate was over. Sadly, Amy moved to another suburb the next year and our relationship was never able to progress into the first grade. Even more tragic, this is when I peaked romantically for the next twelve years.

The next decade would prove difficult.

In the third grade, I had a crush on Carrie. She was forty-five pounds of pure magic and a redhead. Carrie crushed my heart on Valentine's Day when she snubbed me during the card exchange.

I took it hard. In middle school, I developed a crush on Holly. It took a year before I found the courage to have a friend tell her that I liked her. She cried that day. I couldn't imagine it was me. I hoped it was the onset of menstruation that led to her emotional upheaval, but still, it hurt. I did go to the eighth-grade dance with Stephanie, but real romance was hard to find. In high school, I had a lot of crushes on a lot of girls. On Valentine's Day my freshman year, I took a risk and used the student council flower delivery service to send seven flowers to seven people. I received one. It was from me. This led to a wild love affair with Little Debbie, the snack cake. After gaining close to fifty pounds my freshman year in high school, there was more of me to love, but few takers looking to love me. I stopped trying to find a date and took a brief respite from the emotional minefield. For the next eighteen months, I focused on me. I wanted to see how good I could get. It was a personal challenge. I lost sixty-five pounds, got in shape, and got involved in extracurricular activities. I put myself in more rooms with more people and had more experiences. That's when things changed. It was on a bus ride in Toronto during a high school field trip that my luck would turn. I hung out with a girl named Julie most of the trip. We laughed, toured, and sat next to each other as our bus wound through the streets of Toronto. One night, on the dark bus, we French kissed in the English-speaking part of Canada. We never dated, but it was a seed of hope after a very long dry run.

My love life would change forever during my senior year of high school. Her name was Alexis, and still is. She was a swimmer, student council treasurer, and a homecoming runner-up (not quite the queen, but very close). We were in the variety show together, our high school's major stage production. After rehearsal one afternoon, I invited her back to my place, the same place I still shared with my parents. We watched a movie and hung out. When the moment was right, I leaned over and gave her a kiss. She kissed me back. I then kissed her with much more energy. She then asked me to please not put my tongue so far down her throat. I was embarrassed. But I listened. Then, we fell deeply in love. I loved her more than I loved myself (not hard for a guy who barely liked himself). I had no idea why she loved me and I didn't want to ask her why. I didn't want her to think about it, realize she didn't know either, and then end it.

Our relationship continued through the summer and into the fall of my freshman year in college. She was a senior in high school. As the year progressed, our long-distance relationship started to slowly unravel. We began to grow apart. At our worst, her father compared our relationship to a dying puppy, urging Alexis to shoot the puppy. She took her dad's advice. I was devastated. The relationship was over. The hardest part? While I had experienced love, I had no idea how the hell it all happened or how to find it again.

My college years would be filled with random hookups and a longing to find what I had experienced and lost in high school. What I discovered was that it was easier to hook up in rooms with alcohol and that if I didn't look for it, I'd find it. One particular hookup was supposed to last a couple of weeks. Instead, it lasted two years. Once I graduated, my girlfriend stayed behind to finish her senior year. That relationship ended when my former roommate hooked up with her (we were allowed to see other people, but it still hurt).

A couple of years out of college, love was even harder to find. Life beyond college was spent in fewer rooms with fewer people in them. Then, one night, when I least expected it, I met a girl at a bar who I kind of knew from college. We started to date. A month later, we were saying "I love you." The next month, we planned a trip to Ohio for me to meet her parents. I had a feeling that if I took the trip, I might stay with her forever. It was all moving too fast for me. I wasn't ready to move on to the next phase of my life. She was perfectly attractive, but I didn't know if she was my best choice or my only choice. Until this point, dating wasn't as much about options as it was about fortunate accidents. Something felt very wrong. A week before our trip, I told her, "It's not you, it's me." It really was me. And it wasn't her (note to beautiful women who hear this—it really can be him, not you). She thought I was an asshole. I thought I was an asshole, too, but at least I was an honest asshole. A few weeks later, I tried to get back together with her when I couldn't find anyone better. She refused to talk to me. She wanted nothing to do with me. I understood. And again, I was single and searching.

I spent a lot of time beating myself up, sure that I had let the ONE woman who could love me slip out of my life. I should have hung on to her. I thought about her and my mistake—especially on weekends after going to bars and coming home alone. The irony—I was the advice columnist helping millions of people find answers, yet secretly, I was in the same pain, looking for the same answers.

I needed dating to be about intention and purpose. I wanted

control. I wanted to know that I was with my best choice—not my only choice. I needed to find answers.

NAKED ADVICE ··············▶

READER TAKES THE RISK, AND FINDS LOVE

Dear Harlan,
I wanted to let you know that I took your advice to heart and called up an old friend from high school. I had heard his mom passed away and thought he could maybe use a friend. I had no ulterior motive other than being a friend. We talked and planned to get together. He had to leave town, and our plans were put on hold. To my surprise, around a week or so later he called me to say hello and to let me know that he was okay. That's when I somehow got the nerve to blurt out: "I don't know how you will feel about what I'm going to say, but here it goes. This past week, I couldn't stop thinking about you and can't wait until you come home!" To my utter surprise, he responded with "I have butterflies and perma-grin!" So the moral of my story is: If I hadn't followed your advice and taken the risk, I wouldn't have married my husband this past May! It works—take a chance!
  Success Story

Dear Success Story,
Your letter has also given me a case of perma-grin (a
permanent grin, from ear to ear). You made my night, week,
and year. I'm so happy that I could help you take the risk and
find love.

My Getting Naked Experiment
Part Two

A pink envelope arrived in my mailbox addressed to "Help Me, Harlan!" The letter inside was written on a pink note card that smelled of perfume and had attractive writing to match. The author expressed her concern that she couldn't find a man in New York City. She went through a laundry list of her best qualities. There were undertones of flirtation. It was working. I thought about becoming a pen pal, but she didn't include a return address. Besides, that would be questionable. A few weeks later, a second letter arrived. This time, she asked if the first letter was too much for me to handle. Yes! It was. At this point, I was ready to show up at her door and say, "Hi, it's me, Harlan, I've come to help."

Her letter stuck in my mind. I'd think about it when I was alone at night, after a night at the same bars with the same bad results. Soon, thoughts of her started creeping into my day. Then it occurred to me that if this woman lived in Chicago, I'd probably never talk to her. Even if she were visiting, I wouldn't approach her. I didn't talk to random women. I didn't want to make them uncomfortable. At least that was my excuse. Then I realized this woman was a representation of all women and a much bigger problem I was facing. Certainly, there had to be other women like her passing me by on a regular basis. And I knew from letters guys had shared with me that most of them didn't do the approaching either. So, if I did what most men couldn't do, and talked to women during my daily routine, I could meet someone without having to fly to New York to track down the perfumed pink letter writer with no return address.

At that moment, I made a decision to conduct a personal risk-taking experiment. I would later call this Rejection Research. I wasn't trying to get rejected. I was trying to overcome the greatest obstacle that kept me from taking risks, the fear of rejection. I was using what I knew to help me find the courage to take risks. I appreciated that not every woman I approached would want me, but unless I took the risk, I'd never know. To conduct my experiment, I made a rule. For the next three months, I would talk to every woman who gave me *that* feeling. I gave all the women in the city of Chicago permission to not want me. My only task was to talk to them when I got *that* feeling. No matter what I was wearing, how I looked, or how I felt, I had to do the approaching. I would conduct my research at coffee shops, grocery stores, the gym, sidewalks, red lights, online, on planes, on car rental shuttles, and anywhere I got that feeling. The city of Chicago was my petri dish. What happened next would throw me.

I had some success, but I also got rejected. A lot. I received fake phone numbers, occasional insults, and was ignored online on a regular basis. That said, I did have dramatic success. I went on dates with women way out of my league. When the dates ended, I was obsessed with what I did wrong. If we got physical, I was even more concerned with the mistakes I made. I assumed the problem had to be me—my looks, job, sense of humor, or something I said or did on the date. It was all about me. Each rejection and date gone bad was like a punch in the gut. I gained weight (a reoccurring theme in my life). I started to doubt myself. I let other people define me. I had to stop this risk-taking experiment. I couldn't handle the emotional beating that comes with taking risks and approaching women at will. Just giving women permission to not want me wasn't enough.

Taking risks and getting rejected hurt too much.

I stopped my research and spent the next year taking a break from dating. I needed to recoup. I worked to get more comfortable in my skin. I trained to run a marathon. I lost twenty pounds. I wrote my first book. I found new friends. I distanced myself from old ones. I moved to a new apartment. I was brutally honest with myself. What I did over the course of that year would be something I would later refer to as Training in My Thong. After working to be my personal best, better than I'd ever been in my life, the world got bigger, brighter, and better. No one was out of my league. Some women were taller or shorter than me, but no one was too good for me. Instead of seeing opportunities to get rejected, I saw opportunities to meet people and have new experiences. I had a life independent of women. I had new friends. I was in a place I had never been in my life. Instead of looking for someone to rescue me, validate me, or distract me from the pain of being single, I was looking for someone who would complement me and add to my life. I reemerged and started to date again.

This time it was very different. I was less interested in being wanted and more focused on what I wanted. I got set up. I dated online. I approached random women during my daily routine. When I got rejected, it didn't matter. It was truly their loss. I didn't just think it—I believed it. Until I knew the problem was me, I learned to assume the problem was something outside of me.

Then, one day, I ran into Mailboxes, Etc. to make copies for an up-coming speaking convention. That's when I bumped into a woman who gave me *that* feeling. I wanted to talk to her. I didn't know what I was going to say, but I knew I had to say something to her. I wasn't conducting research—I was just following my instincts. I could have looked creepy or made her uncomfortable, but I wasn't thinking about anything other than approaching this girl who gave me *that* feeling. My heart racing, I walked up to her and said exactly what I was thinking:

"Excuse me, I think I know you from somewhere. Have we met?"

"I don't think so," she responded.

I answered, "Are you from around here?"

She said, "Not really. I used to live here until I was five, and then moved away."

Excitedly I replied, "I can't believe it's you. After all of these years . . . You're so much older and really pretty. Remember me? I'm Harlan."

She smiled. She didn't believe me, but still, she thought I was funny.

I continued, "I have to be honest. I don't actually know you, but if we did know each other, this would be very exciting to meet again after all these years. You know?"

She laughed and didn't run.

For the next fifteen minutes we talked. She told me she had just finished graduate school and was staying in Chicago. She was actu-ally faxing a lease. She mentioned needing a roommate. I jokingly offered. She politely turned me down, although she did comment that our last names began with the same letter, so it could work out if we had monogrammed towels. Knowing I might not see this woman again, I said what I was thinking. Hiding my nervousness, I asked, "Can I give you a call some time?"

She said, "Sure." I got her number.

I would have called her sooner, but I was leaving for a conference the next day. I wasn't trying to play games, I was just busy (she later told me she was pissed that I hadn't called sooner, but was still happy I called). When I got back in town, five days later, I dialed her number. She answered. It was a real phone number. I was thrilled.

We made plans for a date that weekend. On Saturday, I came by her place wearing a new pair of shoes. We walked to dinner and then went to Kingston Mines, a blues club in Chicago. We danced to Sandra Hall (I was a horrible dancer). We had our first kiss on the dance floor during a ridiculous song that wasn't introduced to be romantic. The night ended. We continued to see each other over the next few days. On the third date, I noticed a picture in her living room. My jaw dropped. She was one of the girls I had sent a note to via an online dating service. She had responded using a form letter that said, "This member needs to see a picture before she will respond." I had explained in the e-mail to her that I was a public figure and would be more than happy to send her a picture. She neglected to read that part of my note. Ends up the girl I was falling in love with was the same woman who had ignored me and rejected me months earlier.

We saw each other eight days in a row. They say you shouldn't do that, and they're right. On the ninth day, she said she needed space. I agreed. I needed some space, too. I was more than happy to give it to her (something I would have never done in the past because I would have been too afraid of losing the ONE person who could love me). Knowing I had options, I wasn't looking to crowd her. The next day she called me and wanted to date again. A year and two months later I asked her to marry me. She said yes! We made it a long engagement. Long enough for us to be sure we wanted to make this happen. I wanted to make sure I was her best choice, and that she was mine. A year and two months after getting engaged she said I do.

We got married.

I really like my wife. And I love her, too. In fact, I adore her. We have so much fun together. She's my best choice—not my only choice. We are with each other because we choose to be with each other. I can appreciate that there are thousands of men who would love to be with her, and she chooses to be with me. Honestly, it might even make me work a little harder. On the other hand, she knows there are three women and a guy in Dallas who would like to be with me, and that makes her work a tiny bit harder. We are honest with our feelings and comfortable enough to be vulnerable in our thongs (hers look much better than mine). It's the most honest, caring, and loving relationship I've ever experienced—I'm grateful to have her in my life.

How do I know she's my best choice? How do I know I'm the best choice for her? These questions used to confuse me. Before I was married, I stood in wedding after wedding and wondered how one man could commit to one woman. There were so many who gave me *that* feeling. How could anyone choose one? But then, something happened. I had this experience. I went through this process. I realized that I had options. I also knew and loved myself on an entirely different level. I started to date a lot of women. I soon realized I didn't want everyone (even the hot ones) once I got to know them. I wanted someone who could add to my life—make each day better, make me smile, make me want to be my best, be proud to date me, and want to kiss me and be kissed by me.

The most comforting thought—there will be a lot of other women who give me *that* feeling. And I know there will be other men who give my wife *that* feeling. I trust, and I know, that we both have options. I trust that if we both continue to work to be our best, keep having fun together, and don't hide the things hanging out of our Relationship Thong, we can look at other people who give us *that* feeling, and think, *That's* nice, but I already have what I've been looking for. If not for the countless people who wrote to me, over all these years, especially you, the pink perfumed writer, I never would have taken this journey, never have met my wife, and never have found the secret truth to finding happiness in love, and in life.

We live in a world where thousands of people will want us and millions will not. And now, you can embark on your own Getting Naked Experiment to find the thousands who will. All it takes is one.

NAKED ADVICE · · · · · · · · · · · ➤

ICE CREAM NEVER TASTED SO SWEET

It was Wednesday and I was having a bad night. All I wanted was some ice cream, my comfort food. To my disappointment, they had none in our cafeteria. What I did find was Brian, the new and good-looking manager. I told him about my night,

*how I was having problems with my ex-boyfriend, and how I
really needed my favorite ice cream. He promised he'd have it
waiting for me the next day. Thursday arrived and I was
debating whether or not to take a bus to see my ex and patch
things up. I decided against it. My best friend told me to see
Harlan Cohen, who was performing that night at our college. I
had a good feeling about that night, so I got all dolled up and
headed to the show. Wouldn't you know, as I turned the corner
to the auditorium, I saw Brian setting up a catering for
Harlan's performance. Brian told me he had the ice cream for
me and that I should get it afterward. I then went into the
show. During Harlan's event I asked the question, "Where do
you draw the line between saving a relationship and letting
go?" He responded, "If you have to ask this question, then let
go." It was hard to hear. I didn't want to move on from my ex,
my high school sweetheart, my first serious boyfriend. I made
a pact with myself at that moment that I would let go and
move on for good. After Harlan's performance, he met with
audience members who stuck around and we talked some
more. He encouraged me to let go, try new things, and take
new risks. And I did. After the event, Brian had Ben & Jerry's
Phish Food ice cream as promised (I later learned he bought it
on his own dime). Attached to it was a note that read:*

> Jessica, it's the little things in life that put smiles on
> faces. I hope this puts a smile on yours. Any guy who
> 'doesn't want anything to do with you' is a damn
> fool.—Brian

*I knew he was special. Five years later, he and I are still
together. We've started looking at engagement rings and
houses. If it weren't for Harlan encouraging me to take that
risk and Brian's note, I would have never allowed myself to
date him. Who knows? I might still be stuck in a mediocre
relationship, still wondering if I should get out. Thank you,
Harlan. And Brian, too!*

—**Jess, dating five years**

Dear Jess,
Sweet story. Love it! And of course, you're welcome.

Your Getting Naked Experiment: A Recap

Welcome to your quick reference guide to the Getting Naked Experiment. Use it for yourself and to enlist others to participate in the Getting Naked Experiment. Invite enough people and this will become a Getting Naked Movement.

As you conduct your experiment, visit and become a member of www.gettingnakedexperiment.com, the official Getting Naked site (as opposed to all those imposter sites).

1. EMBRACE THE UNIVERSAL REJECTION TRUTH

Give the world permission to want you and not want you. This means completely accepting and embracing The URT.

2. PLAN YOUR RISK(S)

What risk will you take? A risk can be posting an online profile on an online dating site, talking to someone you've been interested in meeting for a while, or getting involved in a group activity. It can also mean getting out of a bad relationship, telling a partner how you feel, and demanding respect. Once you choose a risk, take a look in the mirror in your Risk-Taking Thong and ask yourself the following questions:

> What makes you uncomfortable about this risk?
>
> What's the worst thing that can happen?
>
> What's the best thing that can happen?
>
> What steps will you take to get comfortable with the uncomfortable before the risk?
>
> What thong do you need to train in and what will be your training plan?
>
> Who are the people in your corner to whom you can turn to get comfortable in your Risk-Taking Thong before taking the risk and know you will be okay no matter what?

If in a Getting Naked Group, turn your questions over to the group. If you don't have a Getting Naked Group or aren't comfortable sharing with your group, use the forums on www.gettingnaked experiment.com to help find answers. Do not hide behind excuses.

3. DEFINE YOUR ROLE AND RISK

Before taking each risk, define your role. Defining your role will make it clear who you are, what you want, and how you will get what you want. Defining your risk will help you put together an action plan. Here are the questions to ask while defining your role and risk:

WHO ARE YOU? WHAT DO YOU WANT?

You are attractive, single, and searching—looking to find someone you can love and who can love you (in your thong). You want to find IT and not have it be a big fortunate accident.

WHAT WILL YOU DO TO GET WHAT YOU WANT?

You will put yourself in rooms, talk to people in rooms, and share experiences in rooms. You will ask friends, family, and people who know you best to help you meet people and hang out in rooms. You will never forget that you have options and deserve to be loved. You will always give people permission to want or not want you. You will take all your risks while fully clothed (or in a thong when appropriate) and while totally sober (that's a blood alcohol level under .08).

REMEMBER: Taking action = Success. The ONLY rule: NO beating yourself up. Never regret following your heart.

4. TAKE YOUR RISK

Take your risks as an individual or as a group. Remember, this is an experiment. The focus isn't being liked or desired (that comes later). This experiment is first and foremost about putting yourself in situations to see who you like and desire. Risks don't have to be romantic at first. They can be about setting up future risks over a longer period of time. For example, one week a risk can be putting yourself in a room with people you don't know as part of a class or activity. The next risk can be talking to someone new in these rooms. The following risk can be inviting the people you've met to do something as a group. If you and the rest of your Getting Naked Group meet people in different rooms, your Getting Naked Group can plan a party and invite the people you've met to hang out in one big room. Call it a Getting Naked Party (but be careful, if the invite makes it to Facebook you could have crowd control problems). The more people in your risk-taking group, the more people you can get together and meet as you continue this experiment.

Remember: You can have alcohol, but limit alcohol to one or two drinks during your risk-taking experiment and party. You can drink as much as you want while planning it.

5. CELEBRATE, REFLECT, AND REPEAT

Following the risk, celebrate that you have the testicles or ovaries to take action. You are a hero. You have already succeeded. You are closer to getting what you want regardless of the results. If you achieved your desired result, reflect on how you got it. Understand how you made it happen so you can make it happen again and again. If you didn't get what you wanted, reflect on your result. Ask three questions:

1. Is the problem me?
2. Is the problem a circumstance that has nothing to do with me?
3. Is it The Universal Rejection Truth?

When you reflect, ask yourself tough questions, ask people who don't give you what you want tough questions, and turn to the people in your corner to help you find answers. Expect to be uncomfortable in your Risk-Taking Thong at times. Plan on discovering new uncomfortable areas that will need work and training. Never stop turning to the people in your corner—family, friends, professionals, fellow naked daters, and members of www.getting nakedexperiment.com.

Once you have reflected, repeat the process. Plan a new risk or the same risk. When you do, find ways to tweak the process so you can get the results you desire. The more you practice this five-step approach, the better you will become. Once you find a date and the love of your life, apply this approach to all risks throughout the relationship. If you find your relationship is solid, take professional, social, and spiritual risks using this model for success. It translates to all risks you will take (I'll save this for the next book).

Your results will be guaranteed. They won't always be guaranteed to produce the results you desire, at first, but you will get results. With proper training and thoughtful risk-taking, you will ultimately get what you desire and so much more.

This Getting Naked Experiment should be fun, but it will also be extremely uncomfortable at times (that's a good thing). But I promise, if you want this to work, it will. Speaking of promises, the three promises you made in the beginning of this book will be crucial to your success. You must always know that you have options, deserve love, and that this can, and will, work.

DO IT IN A NAKED GROUP

Consider conducting your Getting Naked Experiment in a group. Think of it like you would think of dieting in a group, only you will gain another person. Form a Getting Naked Group with co-workers, classmates, friends, or acquaintances. If you're on a college campus, start a Getting Naked Group with your fraternity, sorority, club, or organization. If you don't have access to a group or want to reach out to more naked daters, visit www.gettingnakedexperiment.com. Think of the Web site as Getting Naked Central.

Be prepared, some of you might have an easier time conducting your Getting Naked Experiment than others. Some of you will find results faster. Others of you might need to do more training, take more risks, or change your tactics to get what you want. While you're working to get what you desire, know that there is enough love for everyone.

Have a good time with your Getting Naked Experiment. Enjoy the experience. It's all for the sake of research. Read the book as a group. Challenge each other as a group. Train in your thong in a group (but you don't actually have to wear the thong in the group). Take risks in a group. Work through results in a group. Attend one another's weddings as a group. To help you get started on how you can begin your Getting Naked Experiment solo or in a group, I've included more details below. Please e-mail me and post your questions, victories, and struggles on the Web site. I look forward to being in your corner.

TIPS FOR CREATING A GETTING NAKED EXPERIMENT GROUP

1. All naked daters should read the book and embrace the five steps. If naked daters in your group are not readers, they can download the audio version of the book. I can tuck them in at night and help them wake up with someone in the not-too-distant future.

2. Find positive single people looking for love (no negative naked daters). The more positive naked daters in your group the better the vibe. Constantly seek new naked daters to join your group. As the group evolves, you will find yourself meeting more people in more rooms via connections made through fellow naked daters.

3. Naked daters should get together on a regular basis (weekly or biweekly meetings in person or via online chat are ideal).

4. If you don't have a group or can't put one together, find one by posting a note in the forums via www.gettingnaked experiment.com.

HELP OTHER NAKED DATERS

Once you've achieved your desired results, help others. Stand in their corner. Set them up with friends, help them put themselves in more rooms with more people, and tell them what they need to hear (even if it's painful at times). Share your Getting Naked stories and remind them that they have options, deserve love, and that this can work.

GETTING NAKED GROUP SUGGESTIONS

LOCATION: Plan meetings in a comfortable setting free of distractions and noise
FREQUENCY: Once every two weeks or monthly
GROUP LEADER: Run meetings
WHAT HAPPENS AT A GETTING NAKED GROUP MEETING:

- Celebrate the risk (not just the results).
- Take risks as a group.
- Turn to people in your corner to answer questions and offer support and guidance. Consider inviting a professional to sit in on and facilitate discussion and address questions.

Groups will be forming online at www.gettingnaked experiment.com.

---

10 GETTING NAKED EXPERIMENT TIPS

1. Be patient. Give it weeks, months, or years to work. Take small steps and over time, you will be miles ahead.

2. Start with small risks and work your way up to bigger ones. A small risk can be putting yourself in a new room with new people. A bigger one can be talking to these people.

3. Observe people taking risks. Spend some time watching and listening to people during your daily routine. But try not to stare.

4. Talk to people who have found love. Listen to their stories. Then identify the elements of the five-step approach. You'll start to see patterns that will help reveal more answers.

5. Avoid people who don't encourage you to follow your heart and pursue your passion. Quietly distance yourself from them. You don't need them in your corner.

6. Take breaks—this can be emotionally grueling. Work on training in your thong between risks.

7. Do it as a group—get a friend or two to do this with you. It's even easier to have someone else to lean on.

8. Think of this as an experiment. When you call something an experiment it becomes far less emotional—it's research!

9. Try different risks with different people in different situations. Taking a variety of risks will help you go through this process in many different roles and get comfortable in a variety of thongs.

10. Never stop. Once you find the love of your life, use this same approach to taking other risks that come along with living a passionate life. It will work.

If you have a question, post it on www.gettingnakedexperi ment.com or send it to me at harlan@helpmeharlan.com, subject: Getting Naked Experiment. I will post your questions (anonymously) and answer them on the site for everyone else to read and offer advice and insight. I might even use your questions in my advice column and future Naked books.

GETTING NAKED FAQs

WHO IS GETTING NAKED INTENDED FOR?

This book is intended for everyone—single, dating, divorced, widowed, married, and people in complicated relationships. It's for people who are heterosexual, homosexual, bisexual, queer, and transgendered. The themes addressed in the book are universal and resonate with everyone of all ages from eighteen to ninety-eight.

HOW WAS THIS BOOK WRITTEN?

This book is based on a composite of letters written to my advice column over the years, interviews conducted while traveling the country, and conversations with people over the years (many who are experts in their field). The stories and quotes in this book have been collected through an online survey and personal interviews. The Help Me, Harlan! advice sections are based on real letters written to my advice column over the years. The letters have been changed to reflect the broadest themes. Visit www.helpmeharlan .com or contact your local newspaper to read letters from my column. Many of the names attached to the letters have been changed at the request of contributors.

HOW CAN WE COMMUNICATE WITH YOU?

I want to hear from you. In fact, I'd love to hear from you. I intend to write a follow-up book to this that addresses your questions, concerns, victories, challenges, and feedback to encourage other people to go on their journey. You can submit letters via e-mail to harlan@helpmeharlan.com, subject: Getting Naked or via www.gettingnakedexperiment.com. You can also submit feedback through my Help Me, Harlan! Web site: www.helpmeharlan.com.

HOW CAN WE BRING YOU IN TO DO A LIVE PRESENTATION?

Thank you for asking! When I'm not writing, I'm speaking to groups and organizations across the United States and around the world. I'd love to bring the Getting Naked Movement to your community. You can find information about my Getting Naked workshops and other speaking presentations by visiting www.helpmeharlan.com and www.gettingnakedexperiment.com. I also work with several speaking agencies.

HOW CAN WE ATTEND A LIVE GETTING NAKED WORKSHOP OR SEMINAR?

Register for my newsletter at www.gettingnakedexperiment.com or www.helpmeharlan.com.

HOW CAN WE GET YOUR HELP ME, HARLAN! ADVICE COLUMN?

Help Me, Harlan! is distributed by King Features Syndicated and appears in newspapers and on Web sites around the world. You can find out more information by visiting www.helpmeharlan .com or King Features Syndicate (www.kingfeatures.com).

HOW CAN WE FOLLOW YOU ONLINE?

Great question! Here's how to find me. As more social networking sites pop up, I'll be on them. I'm very social.

Facebook: www.facebook.com/helpmeharlan
Twitter: www.twitter.com/harlancohen #GettingNaked
Google+:   www.google.com/harlancohen
Youtube: www.youtube.com/harlancohendotcom
Web site: www.helpmeharlan.com
               www.gettingnakedexperiment.com
               www.nakedroommate.com
               www.happiestkidoncampus.com
               www.dadspregnant.com

E-mail: harlan@helpmeharlan.com

DO YOU PLAY MUSIC? HOW CAN WE LISTEN TO IT?

Wow! How would you even know to ask this question? Amazing. Yes, I do play the guitar and sing original songs. I have an album titled *Fortunate Accidents*. Some of the songs include: "Girl Walks Bye," "The Syphilis Song," and "The Chlamydia Jive." In fact, "The Chlamydia Jive" has been called the best jive since Clapton's version of "The Hand Jive." By who, I'm not sure. The album is available on iTunes, CDBaby, Amazon, and other online stores.

NAKED ACKNOWLEDGMENTS

To my wife and best naked date ever, Stephanie, thank you for loving me, not rejecting me, and always standing in my corner. I adore you. Thank you to Eva Kaye and Harrison, may you always live in a world of endless options. I promise to never offer you dating advice (unless you ask, or *really* need it). To my parents, Eugene and Shirlee, thank you for always encouraging me, believing in me, and reminding me how incredibly handsome and smart I am when I feel uncomfortable in my thong. I love you. Thank you to my big brothers, Vic and Mike, for giving me a front-row seat to dating, relationships, and rejection. I've learned so much from your love, loss, and life experiences. Love you guys so much. To my sister-in-law Irene, love and thanks to you for being there during my single years (and married years). Thanks for always listening and laughing (with me, not at me). Thank you to Marvin and Francine for being the best in-laws a son-in-law could ever want or desire. You could make my life so miserable, but you don't. I love you for that and so many other things. Thank you to my brother-in-law Dan and sister-in-law Rozi for always being so loving, encouraging, and supportive. To Phoebe, Rae, Henry, and Ethan, may you always demand and command respect (and if you don't, your Uncle Harlan will be there to remind you). Thank you to my agent, Eliot Ephraim, for always being in my corner, helping me find the best partners to stand in my corner, and helping me get comfortable in my professional thong (he didn't actually see me in my professional thong). Thank you to Dan Weiss, publisher-at-large at St. Martin's Press, for supporting this Naked adventure and putting together the very best possible team. To my extraordinarily talented editor, Vicki Lame, thank you for making this book the best it can be, encouraging me to be the best I can be, and helping me get even more comfortable in my writing thong. To JJ (Sarah Jae-Jones) for everything you've done throughout this process (so much of which I'll never know). An audible thank-you to Mary Beth Roche, Bob Van Kolken, Laura Wilson, and the entire team at Macmillan Audio. A very special thank-you to Dominique Raccah, Peter Lynch, and the entire team at Sourcebooks for your continued support. Thank you to Glenn Mott, George Haeberlein, Rose McAllister Croke, Claudia Smith, Tiffany Palma, Amy Anderson, and the entire editorial, sales, and management team at King Features Syndicate. Naked gratitude goes out to all the newspaper editors who run Help Me, Harlan!, have run Help Me, Harlan!, or are thinking about running Help Me, Harlan! Heartfelt Naked thanks go out to all the readers who have written to my column, read my column, and shared stories throughout the years in my column. This book is the ultimate answer. A special thank-you to everyone who has hosted my speaking events, attended my speaking events, or thought about attending my speaking events (why didn't you come?). A profound Naked thank-you to all the people who participated in this Getting Naked book and survey (I'd mention everyone's names who completed a Getting Naked Survey, but then you wouldn't be anonymous). Thank you so much!!! Naked thanks to: *Indiana Daily Student*, New York *Daily News*, Indiana University School of Journalism, Purdue University, Ann

Landers, Dr. David Adams, Michael Evans, David Astor, Rachel Martin, Kelly Hagler, Betsy Shirey, Michael Lazerow, Carole Roth, Jason Seiden, Troy Henikoff, Geoff Brown, Michael Brumm, George Benge, Krishnan Anantharaman, Patrick Combs, Sharna Marcus, Lisa Jimenez, Rachel Burstein, Angie Perzanowski, Jessica Levo, Jay Leno, Regina Ackerman, Alexis Del Cid, Jack Canfield, Mark Victor Hansen, NACA, NODA, NASPA, FYE, The Bacchus Network, ACUHO-1, AFLV, and everyone who reads these acknowledgments (you deserve some acknowledgment, too).

ABOUT THE NAKED AUTHOR

◄ • ►

Harlan Cohen is a *New York Times* bestselling author of five books, a professional speaker, and a nationally syndicated advice columnist. He is author of *Getting Naked: Five Steps to Finding the Love of Your Life (While Fully Clothed & Totally Sober), The Naked Roommate: And 107 Other Issues You Might Run Into in College, The Happiest Kid on Campus: A Parent's Guide to the Very Best College Experience (for You and Your Child), The Naked Roommate's First Year Survival Workbook, Dad's Pregnant Too!,* and *Campus Life Exposed: Advice from the Inside.* Harlan has been a guest on hundreds of radio and television programs, including the *Today Show.* He is a professional speaker who has visited more than four hundred college campuses. He is also a singer/songwriter best known for "The Syphilis Song." You can find his books, advice, and music by visiting www.helpmeharlan.com. You can reach Harlan by e-mail at harlan@helpmeharlan.com. Harlan lives in Chicago, Illinois, and is married to his wife, who rejected him via an online dating site before falling in love with him following an unexpected encounter at Mailboxes Etc.